PRAISE FOR

Mass 101

Liturgy and Life

It takes a special kind of genius to research and understand first-rate scholarly insights on a particular topic and then translate those insights into images and language accessible to nonspecialists.

—**FR. J. MICHAEL JONCAS,**

THEOLOGIAN, LITURGICAL COMPOSER,
PROFESSOR, SPEAKER, AND AUTHOR

Emily Strand has seamlessly woven together history, theology, rubrics, meaning, and pastoral wisdom about the eucharistic celebration. Catechists, RCIA leaders, youth ministers, and more can learn from this master catechist.

—**BERNADETTE GASSLEIN,**

EDITOR, *WORSHIP*

Mass 101 is clearly written, informative, and complete. It's the best book on the Mass for Catholic readers this reviewer has come across in quite a while.

—**MITCH FINLEY,**

AUTHOR OF MORE THAN
THIRTY BOOKS FOR CATHOLICS

Mass 101

Liturgy and Life

EMILY STRAND, MA

Liguori

Imprimi Potest:
Harry Grile, CSsR, Provincial
Denver Province, The Redemptorists

Imprimatur: "In accordance with c. 827, permission to publish has been granted on September 27, 2013 by the Most Reverend Edward M. Rice, Auxiliary Bishop, Archdiocese of St. Louis. Permission to publish is an indication that nothing contrary to Church teaching is contained in this work. It does not imply any endorsement of the opinions expressed in the publication; nor is any liability assumed by this permission."

Published by Liguori Publications
Liguori, Missouri 63057

To order, call 800-325-9521 or visit liguori.org

Library of Congress Cataloging-in-Publication Data

Strand, Emily K. (Emily Katherine), 1976-
 Mass 101 : liturgy and life / Emily Strand.—First edition
 pages cm.
 I. Title.
 BX2230.3.S77 2013
 264'.02036—dc23
 2013006377

p ISBN: 978-0-7648-2225-4
e ISBN: 978-0-7648-6862-7

Liguori Publications, a nonprofit corporation, is an apostolate of The Redemptorists. To learn more about The Redemptorists, visit Redemptorists.com.

Printed in the United States of America
19 18 17 16 15 / 6 5 4 3 2
First Edition

Contents

Dedication
For Jude

~

Introduction

This book is intended for anyone who wishes to know more about the Mass: that ancient, most essential act of the Catholic Church. Particularly, it is for those who attend Mass on a regular basis or who feel called to attend Mass and want to know what to expect. It is most especially for those who wish to make their participation in the Mass—whether as music minister, lector, extraordinary minister of holy Communion, or as a member of the praying assembly—more meaningful.

All that could or should be said about the Mass and its meaning is not to be found within these pages. This book only hopes to provide a solid start to developing a better sense of why and how Roman Catholics gather to pray. Perhaps the most valuable notion about the Mass to take away from this volume is an idea of its profundity—its endless wealth of significance that no one book has or will ever fully capture. If this book inspires its reader to find out more about the Mass, it will have fulfilled its purpose.

Although only one name appears on the cover of this book, many people conspired to bring it to you. Allow me to express my thanks to the following people for the support they gave this project and its grateful author:

To Luis Medina, Christy Hicks, and all the good people at Liguori Publications.

To various scholars, colleagues, and friends who took the time to read and comment on the content of this book as it was created, particularly: Dr. Maureen Tilley; Dr. William Johnston; Fr. Gerald T. Chinchar, SM; James Pera; Fr. Steve Walter; Karen Kane; and especially to Jeremy Helmes, who read several chapters and offered great ideas for enhancements to the text, and to Emily Besl, who read the entire manuscript and gave both encouraging and challenging feedback.

To the undergraduate music ministers at the University of Dayton—past, present, and future—for skipping through liturgical history with me.

To Jim Pera again, for always egging me on.

To various family and friends who offered much-needed support for this part-time author (and full-time mom).

To my parents for giving me the gift of faith, a love of liturgy, and the instinct to cling to the Church.

To my husband and especially my son, for sleeping so well while his mother wrote, and

To Fr. Clarence Joseph Rivers, for inspiration to last a lifetime, and then some.

To all these folks and more, I am, like the saints on the morning of the great resurrection, eternally grateful.

EMILY STRAND, MA
COLUMBUS, OHIO
SOLEMNITY OF THE EPIPHANY
OF THE LORD, 2013

CHAPTER 1
Lex orandi lex credendi

WHY LEARN ABOUT THE MASS?

Since the earliest days of the Christian religion, before the Scriptures were composed or the doctrines of the faith were articulated, before the hierarchy of the Church was formally determined, and before any dedicated Church structure was built, Christians gathered to celebrate the Eucharist. The Constitution on the Sacred Liturgy (*Sacrosanctum Concilium*) from the Second Vatican Council tells us the Church has never not come together to celebrate the mystery of our faith: the paschal mystery.[1] This sacred act—this movement of procession, proclamation, profession, and paschal banquet we call "Mass"—is written on the very heart of the body of Christ. As Catholics, Mass is what we do.

Those of us called "cradle Catholics" feel the Mass in the marrow of our bones. Our gestures of participation are instinctual, comfortable, and automatic. (I have an aunt who once blessed herself in the perfume fountain at a department store, only to be informed by a sales clerk, when she looked up in embarrassment, that she wasn't the first Catholic to do so.) The words of our prayers and responses roll off our tongues. New converts and those who inquire into the faith are sometimes intimidated by cradle Catholics' deep-rooted, seemingly inherited familiarity with the Mass, but soon they, too, enter their own intimacy with the Catholic way of worship. Their hearts are drawn to this celebration, and the sounds, smells, and signs of the Mass quickly become part of the fiber of their flesh, the substance of their souls. Soon cradle Catholics and converts alike share the unifying consolation of this ancient, ingrained, and established way of praying.

So why learn about the Mass? Why disturb the peace and comfort of our happy ritual home? What will happen when we break open this mystery of our faith to see what's inside? What if we find something ironic, something we don't expect? What if learning about the Mass only leads us to more questions, only deepens the mystery before us?

Perhaps the best entry point into the answer to this important question is through a very old Latin axiom that has come down through the ages of our tradition, bearing rich meaning for both our worship and our identity as Church: *lex orandi lex credendi*. The phrase literally means "the law of prayer is the law of belief." The idea this phrase represents first appeared in a fifth-century letter to Pope Celestine I, reportedly written by a lay monk called Prosper of Aquitaine, who was a disciple of the renowned bishop and doctor of the Church, St. Augustine.

Both Prosper of Aquitaine and his teacher St. Augustine lived in a time in Church history that was crowded with controversy. Four hundred years or so after the life, death, resurrection, and ascension of Christ, the Church was still working to articulate the doctrines of faith that follow from the teachings and actions of Jesus. The immediate influence of those who had been close to Jesus in his life and ministry was gone from the world. At the same time, the persecution of the early Church was for the most part over. Out of such circumstances, pastoral questions arose with no easy answers, such as, "Should the children of Christians be baptized at birth or later?" Answering these questions through theological scrutiny usually led to deeper, more fundamental questions, such as, "how significant is original sin?" and "is our salvation initiated by us or God?" St. Augustine, with the aid of scholars like Prosper of Aquitaine, spent much of his time and all of his formidable faculties for logical thinking and rhetoric working out the "orthodox" (literally: "right-believing") answers to these important questions of faith and writing them down. In so doing, they helped build the theological framework of our faith.

The letter containing the idea in question, *lex orandi lex credendi*, was part of a conversation aimed at clearing up just such a controversy of belief or heresy. The heresy at hand was begun by the theologian Pelagius, who downplayed and even denied our need for God's grace to perform good works or even to take the first steps toward salvation. Eventually the Church (with significant help from St. Augustine) authoritatively articulated the orthodox position on the matter: that our salvation is wholly and entirely due to God. God even plants in us the desire to be saved in the first place, and we turn toward God for salvation as a result of this God-given desire, much like the way a sunflower's face is drawn toward the sun.

In his letter to Pope Celestine I, Prosper of Aquitaine made a new yet convincing point for the side of orthodoxy on this issue. He pointed to the way the Church *prays* as a means of revealing how the Church *rightly believes*. The liturgy, well-established and celebrated by the entire Church everywhere, gives testimony to the orthodox belief that God initiates our salvation through grace. Liturgy, claimed Prosper of Aquitaine, does this by means of the Intercessions, or the Prayer of the Faithful. At each Mass, the assembly prays these Intercessions, rooted in the exhortations to prayer in St. Paul's First Letter to Timothy, for various needs, one of which is always for the salvation of the world. Thus, concluded Prosper, in our established tradition of worship we find evidence of our established belief: Salvation is from God alone. If we did not believe it was God who initiated our salvation through grace, why would we pray each Sunday for the world to be saved by God? This is evidence of our belief that we have no power to enact the world's salvation, and that power belongs solely to God. And so, he suggested, let the law of prayer establish the law of belief: *lex orandi lex credendi*.[2]

Prosper of Aquitaine's argument was innovative but not really new; the Church's liturgy is and has always been a source of apostolic authority. The apostles themselves, among others, were the first worshipers of the risen Christ, and more importantly, it was Christ himself who taught his Church how to pray through his example of prayer and his establishment of the Eucharist. The early liturgies of the nascent Church are, in many instances, thought to be a content source for the New Testament Scriptures, which record not simply prescriptions for how liturgy should be done but accounts of what was already taking place in the earliest gatherings of Christians. So it was natural, in the heresy-laden patristic era in which Prosper and his mentor Augustine wrote, for the liturgy to serve as a bulwark of orthodoxy.

Time has not eroded the patristic Church's reverence for liturgy as the guardian of its most essential beliefs. The modern Church goes even further, viewing liturgy as both the source and summit of the Christian life. This understanding of ritual as absolutely essential to Catholic religious belief and practice confirms sociological understandings of the role ritual plays in human culture. In his book *Catholics and American Culture*, author Mark Massa connects Prosper's ancient axiom with the more modern ideas of Émile Durkheim. Durkheim, the father of modern sociological study, viewed ritual as the point at which our religious ideas and beliefs become a real, tangible part of our human experience. God is an abstraction to humans without ritual, which provides the believer a point of encounter with the divine.[3] The action-oriented nature of religious ritual is where, Durkheim says, a community of believers becomes aware of itself and its place. It is only through the ritual gestures and acts it undertakes that such a community is able to hold collective ideas and shared sentiments.[4] Massa reminds us that Durkheim's ideas on the *ritual actions* of a religion founding and shaping the *theological ideas* of a religion, though they represent a break with other social theorists of his day, are but a social-scientific rehashing of Prosper of Aquitaine's famous instruction on the importance of liturgy.[5]

But why? What makes liturgy wield such influence in our lives, both individually and collectively? And what are the collective ideas and shared sentiments that Durkheim claims our Catholic ritual symbolizes? How could one hour of our week on Sunday morning (or evening, or Saturday afternoon) really sum up everything we believe? How could Mass be, as the modern Church upholds, the truest expression of the Christian life? These are all questions we begin to answer when we take time to learn more about the mystery we celebrate each week in the holy Eucharist—when we break out of our ritual comfort zones to investigate our worship's deeper meaning. And in so doing, the faithful (and perhaps comfortable) Mass-goer enters into a new level of participation in the Church and in the Christian life itself. God, through Christ, invites us not just into his Church but into his life: a life in the Spirit that calls us to greater personal holiness, loving union with one another, and to the healing of the world. And the path toward fully embracing this paschal mystery to which we are called is and has always been through the shared sacraments of the Church Christ founded, especially the Eucharist.

Now let's face it—sometimes the hour we put in at Church on the weekend is not the most inspiring of our week. Homilies can limp, the music isn't always very good, or a toddler's antics in the next pew can distract us from being fully present to prayer. But something else may make it difficult, even impossible, to be fully present to the mystery we celebrate: lack of understanding. I have never been a fan of American football. In fact, I don't even know or understand the rules of the game. This makes my experience of watching even the most exciting game of football torturously boring. I get absolutely nothing out of it because I have no idea what's going on. But this isn't the fault of the game itself. I get nothing out of watching football because I put nothing into the experience—I haven't even bothered to learn how it works or what it's all about. Until I do, the experience of watching it will continue to be meaningless for me. So it is with Mass, the history, complexity, and deeply symbolic nature of which beg for lifelong consideration by its participants. And best of all, learning about liturgy by those who celebrate it (that is, all of us) results in more beautiful, more solemn, more graceful, and more fulfilling experiences of liturgy for the entire assembly. Of all reasons, this seems the best one for learning more about the Mass. If Mass is the sacrifice we offer God in thanksgiving for his great gift to us in Jesus Christ, shouldn't our expression of Mass be as good, graceful, and beautiful as possible? Shouldn't we enter into it as fully as we are able? Learning more about what we do on Sundays can help us with this lofty yet worthy goal.

LEITOURGIA

Once we are resolved to know more about the Mass, where do we begin? A good starting point may be to examine the nature and purpose of our worship. What is liturgy, and why do we take part in it?

The word "liturgy" comes from a Greek word, *leitourgia*, which refers to public works, or infrastructure: roads and bridges, plumbing and other structures that give support to the workings of a society. And like these support structures for society, Christian liturgy supports the body of Christ. Without gathering to worship, the Christian Church has no real form or shape, no communal identity or ideas. But we do not celebrate liturgy merely for our own sakes; it does not exist to "prop up" the Church as an institution in itself. Rather, liturgy is the infrastructure for the body of Christ's relationship with the Triune God.

What does it mean for a relationship to have an infrastructure? Some relationships have strong infrastructure, some weak, but without the support that infrastructure provides, there is no hope for a relationship's survival. If you have ever been in a romantic relationship, it probably began with dating. Dating provides the infrastructure of quality time and shared experiences on which a couple builds and sustains a relationship. The building phase is natural and easy for most couples: sharing time, interests, creating memories. I met my husband while I was in graduate school, and I remember looking so forward to weekend dates with him, I could barely concentrate on my studies during the week. But later in many relationships, when the initial passion of new love has cooled, sustaining the infrastructure of the relationship becomes more challenging. A married couple lives together and sees much of each other throughout their days or evenings, but these fleeting moments of togetherness, dominated by housekeeping and parenting responsibilities, do not sustain a relationship. The couple must resolve to spend quality time together, which often means giving form or structure to the time they share through planned activities: a neighborhood walk, dinner at a special restaurant, or simply sharing a glass of wine while discussing the day. Sharing time for companionship is how each member of the couple communicates to the other that time together is both a priority and a pleasure. It also creates new shared memories and keeps the relationship expanding instead of contracting.

Infrastructure is essential to romantic relationships, but the same is true of relationships between friends. I have a friend with whom I really enjoy spending time, but we are so busy we hardly ever get together. We usually get stuck in the scheduling phase of sharing time together, then dust settles on the last e-mail exchange and weeks or months go by before I realize we never met up. I feel us becoming more distant, more ignorant of each other's current circumstances, joys, and struggles.

How long can this go on before we cannot really call ourselves "friends" anymore? Maybe she will become "someone I used to know." Perhaps you have been to a grade school, high school, or college reunion, only to find people you were great friends with in the past have now become strangers, not only because of their changed appearance but because they are living lives with which you have no connection, no knowledge. Social networking sites provide some means of infrastructure for people's continued relationships. But with no infrastructure at all, relationships die.

In this same way, infrastructure is essential to the body of Christ's relationship to God, and liturgy is the form this infrastructure takes. In a sense, the celebration of the Mass is our all-important weekly "date" with God. Again, this is not simply for us; God wants desperately to be close to us, to celebrate with us, to share sacred time with us. This is why, in the Book of Exodus, God initially sets into motion his plan for the rescue of the Hebrews from slavery in Egypt. The Hebrews cry out to God in their distress, and he hears them and wishes them to be free to worship him in the desert, something they were not able to do in their captivity. The Lord instructs Moses to say to Pharaoh: "Thus says the LORD: Israel is my son, my firstborn. I said to you: 'Let my son go, that he may serve me'" (Exodus 4:22–23a). Over and over this desire of God to be worshiped by his people is repeated throughout Exodus.

For some, it may be tempting to think of God's desire to be worshiped as characteristic of some megalomaniacal deity who wants his creatures fawning obsequiously over him. But a deeper consideration shows Israel's worship must have been more than an ingratiating display of piety. Worship in the desert removed the Hebrews from the fast pace and rampant corruption of the cities in which they labored. It gave them a much-needed respite from their work and even allowed them to spend time with their immediate and extended families and to celebrate and strengthen their cultural identity as the people of God. So while worship was not simply for the sake of the Hebrews, at the same time worshiping God in the desert must have been one of the deepest desires of their hearts, one that made them dream of freedom and inspired their cries to God for liberation. And these cries God answered in ways the Hebrews couldn't have dreamed possible. Worship, therefore, is a two-way street: a mutually desirable activity for both parties in the relationship.

Liturgical or Devotional Prayer?

But why must liturgy be the form the infrastructure of our relationship with God takes? Most people in relationships will tell you it doesn't matter what a couple does together as much as simply being together. Isn't it so in our relationship with God?

Yes and no. Yes, God wants to be with us. He wants our everyday prayers, our thoughts, our frustrated cries for help, our moments of joy in our daily living. God wants us to take at least a few moments out of every day for reflection on the Scriptures, to say the rosary over our morning coffee, or even to sing spontaneous hymns of joy in the shower. These moments help sustain a relationship between us as individuals and God. It is called devotional prayer. In her book *The Ministry of Music*,[6] Sr. Kathleen Harmon explains devotional prayer is formed out of our own, individual, immediate needs. Its form changes as our needs change. Devotional prayer can take many forms: more structured forms such as the rosary, or it can simply consist of spontaneous conversation with God. A friend from high school, an accomplished ballet dancer, once told me she liked to dance to express her prayers and her love for God. This is devotional prayer.

Liturgical prayer, especially the celebration of the Eucharist, is something very different. Sr. Harmon explains that liturgy, unlike devotional prayer, is not formed by our own needs and desires in the moment but rather *forms us* into the body of Christ and enters us into the paschal mystery of Christ. We know Jesus desired "that they may all be one," even as he is one with his Father in heaven (John 17:21). Becoming the body of Christ through sharing the Eucharist both makes us one, fulfilling Christ's wish, and gives us the power to become one body outside the doors of the Church: in our hearts, in our actions, in our love for all people. And the paschal mystery is the story of both Christ and his body the Church. As Christ died and rose, so the Church dies and rises every day. But we have no idea what this story of dying and rising means—though it means so much more than all the world—if we do not participate in it through the one, unique way Christ intended when he instituted the Eucharist. So when my friend from high school dances to pray instead of attending Mass on Sunday mornings, this is something akin to eating oranges for protein in your diet. Devotional prayer, although important to each believer's relationship with God, cannot do what liturgy does. Liturgy makes us one body, broken and shared for the salvation of the world.

CAUTION: LEARNING ABOUT LITURGY WILL CHANGE YOU

I hope you are already gleaning a sense from this book that there is much about the Mass you have yet to consider. If so, you are in for a profound experience. Learning about the Mass is fascinating for believers because Mass, as you may already be coming to understand, is like a microcosm of our entire faith. But learning about Mass can also be unsettling. Discovering more about why Catholics pray together the way we do, the history behind Mass and the Church's sometimes specific, sometimes open-ended instructions for how to conduct our prayer can challenge long-held opinions or preferences and make old habits less comfortable.

For nearly ten years I was blessed to minister to Catholic university students as they grew in knowledge and appreciation of the liturgy they helped lead as liturgical ministers. I could usually predict their initial reaction to the new information and understanding they gleaned in their first semester of intense liturgical studies: *disorientation*. Previous ideas and misconceptions fell away as they studied the ancient liturgical traditions of the Church and more recent directives on liturgy set forth by the Vatican and regional bishops. The crisis of their learning usually came to a head when they traveled home for breaks and experienced the setting of worship in which they were raised through their new lens of liturgical study. They were often scandalized by practices they had once thought nothing of, and sometimes they were pleased, inspired, and emboldened by some element of their parish worship they had always taken for granted. In almost every case, these newly informed students saw, heard, sang, and prayed the liturgy with new eyes, new ears, new voices, and new hearts.

Best of all, these young people, these new liturgical scholars, often began to contribute to the liturgy wherever they worshiped, with great passion for helping the assembled body of Christ express and enter into the paschal mystery in ways more faithful to our Church's long tradition of prayer. Above all, this is the *telos* (Greek for ultimate purpose or truest aim) of all liturgical study: not to change individuals (though it can do that) but to change the way we worship. In the worship of the body of Christ on earth, there is always room for improvement. We can always grow, always become more graceful, more gracious, and more beautiful in the way we pray. We can always seek more meaning out of the gestures and words we use for worship. All is not relative when it comes to the Church at prayer, and growing in knowledge of the liturgy we celebrate is the perfect antidote to complacency in our worship. Most importantly, if this Mass we celebrate is a microcosm of our whole tradition, if the law of praying really is the law of believing, then by more beautifully becoming the body of Christ, by entering more fully into the paschal mystery, we will come closer to fulfilling Christ's prayer that all may be one and his command to do this in memory of him.

DISCUSSION QUESTIONS

1. What does the phrase **lex orandi lex credendi** *mean, and what insights does the phrase bring to our understanding of worship?*

2. *Why does the Church view its ancient tradition of worship as a source of orthodoxy or right-believing?*

3. *How could lack of understanding inhibit our experience of worship? How could growth in understanding change our experience?*

4. *What does the word* **liturgy** *literally mean, and what does that tell us about the purpose of liturgy?*

5. *In what ways is liturgy like our "date" with God? Do you think this is an appropriate comparison? Why or why not?*

6. *What is the difference between liturgical prayer and devotional prayer? Why does this difference matter?*

7. *Why can learning more about the Mass be unsettling? What do we stand to gain by learning more about the Mass?*

CHAPTER 2
Why We Pray This Way:
The Historical Context of the Mass

The best way to get to understand people is to discover their story: Where did they come from? How did they come to be where they are now? What struggles and challenges have they met along the journey? Discovering the answers to such questions helps you understand who they are now and what inspires them to feel, act, think, and relate the way they do. Knowing their stories will often help you connect more deeply with people out of compassion for them or through shared experiences.

The same can be said of the Mass. This ancient act of prayer that we celebrate each Sunday has a long, rich, and fascinating past. Knowing something of the historical context of the Mass helps those of us who celebrate it make a stronger connection with the way we worship and even with the saints and all the faithful who celebrated it long before us.

The story of the Mass begins with another story, from chapter 24 of Luke's Gospel, about the disciples encountering Jesus on the road to Emmaus. In a way, this story gives us the earliest model of Christian worship and shows us the centrality of Christ therein. In the story, the disciples meet the risen Jesus on the road—though his identity is hidden from them—and he interprets the Scriptures for them. Then he joins them in a meal, and in the blessing and breaking of the bread they recognize him as the Christ, but upon this recognition he disappears from their sight. In this ancient and beautiful story, we see the early shape and character of Christian liturgy: a simple yet profound sharing of the Word and meal of thanksgiving in which Christ himself is present, though in a shrouded and mysterious way.

How then did the worship of the Christians progress as it moved into a post-ascension world? What characterized the Mass in the early centuries of the Church, and how did it grow, change, and develop in the ages that followed?

THE EIGHTH DAY

The Constitution on the Sacred Liturgy (*Sacrosanctum Concilium*) from Vatican II rightly refers to Sunday as the foundation of the entire liturgical year.[7] This parallels the idea that Christ's resurrection is the foundation of the whole Church, for the resurrection is what Sunday stood for to the earliest Christians. This connection between Sunday and the resurrection is firmly established in all the Gospel accounts of Jesus' rising from the tomb. All the evangelists agree this glorious event occurred on the first day of the week, which in the Jewish world was the day after the Sabbath: Sunday.

For the early Church, there was a strong distinction between the Jewish Sabbath and the "Lord's day" of the Christians. In fact they were different days: Sabbath was (and is) observed from sundown Friday to sundown Saturday. Important differences separated them conceptually as well, yet the distinction between them eroded over time and remains weak today. To uncover what Sunday meant and still means for Christians, it is helpful to separate it from the Jewish idea of Sabbath. While both the Jewish Sabbath and the Christian Sunday were times for the community's worship, there was no prohibition from work for Christians on Sunday as for Jews on the Sabbath; Sunday was in fact a normal workday in that time period. Christians would have abided by the Roman pagan culture's workweek, yet they went about their labor knowing that first day of the week was a day outside of time itself. In a seven-day week, Christians called Sunday "the Eighth Day." Sunday was, as Psalm 118 describes, a day made by the Lord: a day for miracles, a day penetrated with the presence of God, who creates the world anew through the resurrection of his Son. The resurrection occurring on the first day of the week recalled for these Jewish-Christians the first day in the creation story of Genesis on which God separates the light of day from the darkness of night; the Christians knew themselves to be called, as the First Letter of Peter professes, out of the darkness of sin and into the wondrous light of life in Christ. Though every day was for living this new life, Sunday was the day to celebrate it and to sustain it through the sharing of the Eucharist. (Early on in Christianity, since days were reckoned to begin with the setting of the sun, Christians' observance of the Lord's day would take place at the earliest "Sunday" opportunity: on Saturday night, but this was soon transferred to Sunday.[8])

This distinction between the Lord's day and the Jewish Sabbath points up an important characteristic of the earliest Christians: their expectation of the end times as imminent. The Gospels record Jesus' many teachings about the end of the world, so it is no wonder his disciples came to expect this end sooner rather than later—in their own lifetimes for certain. The earliest Christians' thoroughly eschatological (from the Greek word *eskhaton* meaning "last" and referring to the last days of the world) outlook shaped everything about their experience and the character of the early Church. For instance, it helps us understand, in part, why the Gospel accounts were not written down for a few generations after the events of Jesus' life, death, and resurrection. Instead they were told orally at Christian gatherings. Among other reasons, it also helps explain why buildings dedicated solely to Christian worship were not erected for the community for generations. When the end of the world is nearly upon us, one does not focus on things and places but on what matters most: living the life given to us in Christ and looking forward to witnessing the fulfillment of God's plan for the cosmos.

Just think of that! How would your life be affected by the knowledge that the end of time was around the corner? Maybe it would happen next Thursday, maybe next year, maybe tomorrow…maybe it is happening already. How would your day-to-day activities change? How would you choose to spend your time, and with whom? Perhaps it is important to note that the early Church's instincts in those first "last days" led them to celebrate the Eucharist. The instinctive actions of a thoroughly eschatological *ekklesia* (St. Paul's term for "Church") were liturgical actions.

So despite the necessity of work on Sundays, the Christians, convinced that any given Sunday might be the day of the Second Coming, found ways to make each Sunday a festival day. In many instances, they would arise before the dawn, before their work began, to celebrate a service of the Word, in which the Scriptures were proclaimed. Then it was off to work, but as the daylight faded and their work obligations released them, they would reconvene for a celebration of the Eucharist, which in the earliest days took place in the context of the main evening meal, though in structure quite recognizable as the ancestor of today's Liturgy of the Eucharist. Later, when a suspecting emperor Trajan outlawed suspicious evening gatherings, and through reform of a eucharistic meal that was becoming too large or extravagant, the Christians combined their Word and Eucharist services into one early-morning celebration, without a main meal. In this combination and simplification of services, the Mass as we know it takes recognizable shape.[9]

SEVEN CHARACTERISTICS OF EARLY CHRISTIAN WORSHIP

Scholars have uncovered much about the early liturgies of the Church. Through ancient writings, archeological findings and other evidence, we can get a sense for how the early Christians worshiped. Let us keep in mind that the early Christian Church was not formally structured and existed in the highly diverse cultural setting of the later Roman Empire. While all Christian communities seemed to follow a basic liturgical model of sharing the Scriptures and breaking the bread, there was diversity in the expression of this model. Therefore, instead of painting too detailed a picture, let us discuss seven important characteristics that all early Christian worship seems to have shared.

1. Early Christian worship was primary and identity-shaping. I have already described that apocalyptic mindset of the first Christians that caused them to turn to corporate prayer as the essential way of expressing their faith in what were, they imagined, the last days of time. Dom Gregory Dix says the Christians' worship, based on the actions of Jesus and the teachings of those who knew him personally, animated the nascent Church both as a corporate body and as individual members.[10] Dix points out the persecution of Christians by the Roman authorities was based not on the holding of Christian beliefs but on an individual's participation in the gathered Church's worship. This points up the essential nature of gathering to celebrate the Eucharist to the identity of Christ's early followers; if you did not gather with others for Christian worship, you could not be found guilty of being a Christian. Celebrating the Eucharist was what sustained them and enabled them to live a Christian life. No other form of prayer or Christian activity, including service to the needy, could compare with the Eucharist in its influence or significance to the early Church.

2. Early Christian worship was pluriform. I may be inventing a word with "pluriform," but to describe liturgy across the early Church, I needed a word that was the opposite of "uniform" without seeming chaotic and scattered. If you were an ancient Christian traveling the world of late antiquity to visit various Christian communities at prayer, you might have felt at home in each. You would also have noted many variations on their expressions of the core rites. Christian worship was, in many places, based upon a simple structure echoing the Jewish synagogue service of the Word and the meal of blessing and thanksgiving that Jesus modeled at the Last Supper. But elements within that simple structure varied from region to region and from community to community. And even the structure itself could vary; Bradshaw and Johnson note that factors such as the means of each community (for example, whether a wealthy person hosted the Eucharist or whether it was a gathering of poor believers) had a significant influence on the shape and content of the gathering itself.[11] Even elements such as the Eucharistic Prayer were fluid, unfixed and usually improvised by the president (the one who presided over the community's prayer; today we call this person the presider), based on an outline of ideas to cover in the prayer. And though most Eucharistic Prayers included Jesus' words of institution from the Last Supper ("this is my body, this is my blood"), even these are absent from some ancient and yet quite orthodox Eucharistic Prayers, such as the very early east-Syrian Anaphora (Eucharistic Prayer) of Addai and Mari.[12] Eventually, in the course of the development of the Christians' prayer, excellent turns of phrase or beautiful and evocative images improvised in prayer would be passed to other communities until a canon of Christian prayer begins to form. But in the earliest days, the worship of these apocalyptic communities was varied and not strictly delineated.

This pluriformity was due in no small part to the marked diversity of that group of people that made up the early Christian Church. Jesus was a Jew, and many of his original followers were Jewish; we can observe that the basic structure of Christian prayer was Jewish. But even as early as the New Testament writings we see issues surrounding diversity becoming very important among the Christians. So the prayer of communities of Christians who were mostly Jewish would have been overwhelmingly influenced by Judaism. But in Gentile Christian communities, the same basic structure of prayer would have been influenced by traditions from the Greco-Roman world with its strong sense of ceremonial (ritual movement, planned corporation action).[13] Where there was a mix of Jewish and Gentile Christians, you guessed it—a mix of traditions converged to inform their worship.

3. *Early Christian worship was done by all.* Earlier I introduced a Greek word, used by St. Paul, to refer to the early Church: the *ekklesia*. This word had staying power and is recognizable as the root of English words like "ecclesial" (relating to church) and "ecclesiology" (the study or theological conception of church). When St. Paul used it to refer to the Christian Church, he was certainly not alluding to church buildings. Rather he was referring to a temple built of people, or as St. Peter puts it, a spiritual house made up of living stones. Therefore, there were no passive spectators in early Christian worship; the celebration of the Eucharist was done by all. Kenneth Stevenson claims hard and fast divisions between ordained and nonordained members of the Christian community are difficult to justify at this stage in Christian history.[14] The reason for having one presider over the liturgy was mostly functional; one person was needed to lead the community's prayer in the place of Christ. And the reception of the Eucharist was also done by all: adults, even small children. All the baptized received Communion.

4. *Early Christian worship was simple.* Dix points out the straightforward nature—the directness—of the ritual act in the early Church, as befits what was then a domestic act conducted in the homes of prominent Christians for the community at large.[15] There were few if any devotional elaborations on the ritual, and Dix supposes the whole service may have taken only twenty minutes from start to finish.[16] But don't think of early Christian celebrations of Mass as akin to a committee meeting. Dix points out any time you have a group of people participating together in a ritual act, some ceremonial is necessary. Their worship was simple, but not for the sake of being simple; don't confuse the early Christians with the Puritans of the sixteenth and seventeenth centuries with their emphasis on plainness of worship and church architecture. For the early Christians, the emphasis was simply on the function of the gathering, which was to perform the essential action of the ritual: the blessing, breaking, and sharing of the Eucharist. Everything else was secondary.

5. *Early Christian worship was action-oriented.* This characteristic of early Christian worship is related to its simplicity. At the heart of the new commandment of Christ was the simple instruction to *do* this—to break the bread, to drink the cup—in memory of him. The simple yet profoundly mysterious transformation of everyday objects like bread and wine into the flesh and blood of Christ, and the transformation of those who partake of these gifts into the body of Christ, were why the Christians gathered. The practice of Eucharistic Adoration (with or without exposition) was not established by the early Christians and would not have made sense to them; it was a much later development. Though early Christians were known to take consecrated elements home with them, the purpose would have been to nourish those who could not participate in person, and to sustain themselves by eating this wondrous food between communal gatherings. Always most important was the *action* of bread and wine becoming Body and Blood, and the Christians' *act* of taking part in this sacrifice. The eucharistic action, and their participation in it, is what drew Christians together, despite the possible consequence of death or life in prison if they were discovered by the Roman authorities. As Christ had sacrificed himself for the forgiveness of the world, so Christians sacrificed themselves to be his body. The early Church's emphasis on action was, in part, an expression of their emphasis on the sacrifice of Christ and the necessity of their own participation in it.

6. *Early Christian worship was sung.* Most people who have studied the history of Jesus' time know he lived in an "oral culture," one that emphasized shared stories over written words. But few people appreciate the overwhelming influence of orality, or a cultural emphasis on sound and speech, on the worship experience of the early Christians. We modern Western people are visually oriented; sight dominates our other senses, and to us, seeing is believing. For the early Christians and their Jewish ancestors, *hearing* would have dominated their way of knowing, understanding, and believing. It wasn't just that books, paper, and ink were too expensive and hard to get. The ancients didn't write their important stories down the way we do today because it wasn't the authoritative way of preserving and transmitting them. As Edward Foley puts it, the primary way of knowing was through auditory events: through sound.[17] This is demonstrated, reports Foley, by the prevailing practice of reading aloud. In late antiquity, even when a person read something alone for only his own benefit, he read it out loud.

This auditory dominance in the culture of the earliest Christians made music entirely inextricable from worship. Today we might celebrate weekday Mass with little to no music, and though this is considered less festive to us, it is not considered strange. Foley says a music-less celebration of Mass would be not just strange but unintelligible to the earliest Christians. Today some parts of Mass are spoken and some are sung. In the earliest Church, distinctions between spoken and sung prayer were not so easy to discern. In fact, the ancient Christians' manner of formal speech would have sounded, to modern ears, like singing. (If you've ever listened to audio recordings of Dr. Martin Luther King, Jr.'s speeches, you are familiar with the way his voice seemed to break into song as his energy level rose and he made an important point. This might give our imaginations some sense of what it sounds like when speech and singing intermix as they must have in the ancient Church's worship.) Similarly, there is no reference, in the earliest centuries of Christian worship, to designated "liturgical musicians" who led the assembly's song. Singing was so integral to celebration, so innate in worshipers, that such leadership was unnecessary. Certain soloists would have chanted the Scriptures or prayers, but the assembly may have at times added their voices to these as well, using well-known musical formulas carried over from Jewish synagogue traditions. Foley claims the emphasis in the new Christian worship was ever on the assembly's united song, and the singing of hymns fostered the musical and spiritual union of those present.[18] So while different types of music, such as chanting and hymn-singing, existed for the earliest Christians as they do for Christian assemblies today, music in the early Church was in general more inherent, more essential to the worship. This inseparability of music from worship in the earliest celebrations of the Eucharist creates challenges for the study of music in the early Mass. But one thing is certain: As Joseph Gelineau said, the Christian Church was born singing and has never stopped.[19]

7. Early Christian worship was persecuted. The first three centuries of Christianity were fraught with violence. The persecution of Christians was linked to the slow but steady decline of the Roman Empire, for empires in decline tend to look for someone to blame, some external source of their troubles. The rapid rise of the Christian Church made some Roman authorities believe that, by their unshakable devotion to the one God of Jesus Christ, the traitorous Christians had brought down the ire of the many Roman gods, throwing the empire into disfavor and bad fortune. Efforts were made to root out Christian communities, and there was no better trap in which to catch them than their gatherings for worship. Meanwhile, Christian worship and other "suspicious" practices garnered the mistrust of the general populace of the empire. The Christians, with their new ways of worship (which were rumored to involve eating flesh and drinking blood), their referring to one another as "brother" and "sister" (were they incestuous?), and their secretive gatherings (furtive for fear of the Roman authorities) quickly became the scapegoat for the fears of the people and the troubles of authorities alike.

The Church's persecution influenced the character of early Christian worship in several significant ways. First it must have bonded the early Christians together. Dix supposes that people who, through their shared activity are risking at least a lifetime of penal servitude and at worst a gory execution in the arena games, tend to get to know their associates.[20] Secondly it gave them a strong—much stronger than we have today—sense of their own part in the mission of the world's salvation, brought to birth by God-in-Christ through his paschal mystery. It taught them that the celebration of the Eucharist, the sharing in Christ's Body and Blood, was the source of this redeemed life and also the height to which redemption takes us on earth. Eucharist was the foretaste of the glory of God to which each believer had a promised share. (One thinks more about his promised share in divine glory when one regularly participates in a "crime" that carried a sentence of death, often carried out on the day of one's arrest.) Thirdly the persecution of the early Church led to unbridled curiosity in Christianity by non-Christians and undoubtedly fueled its rapid rise in those first three centuries. The places where Christians gathered for worship became exceedingly crowded, as architectural evidence at places like Dura Europos, a third-century house church, suggests. The ancient historian Tertullian famously said the blood of those who were martyred for their faith became the seeds of the Christian Church. The followers of Jesus Christ may have begun as a handful of trembling disciples, but by the year 300 they were at least seven million strong.[21]

CONSTANTINE AND THE CHANGING CHURCH

The apparent conversion of the emperor Constantine to Christianity in 312 and the consequent legalization of Christianity brought big (if gradual) change to the character of the Christian Church. First it brought an end to the era of persecution; though bouts of violence against Christians still flared in the generations that followed, the worst was certainly over. This in turn must have brought a change in perspective for the Christians. The Christians had, since the end of the first century, revised their expectation of an imminent return of Christ, but the end of persecution would have softened the urgency of their participation in his body through the sacraments and brought more safe space to express their faith. Christian art and writing could flourish in this less hostile environment, and dedicated Christian houses of worship were springing up to welcome the flourishing Church.

Thirdly the identification of the emperor with Christianity brought more responsibility and power to the leaders of the Christian Church: the bishops, priests, and deacons. Historian Theodor Klauser notes the Church and state went into a sort of partnership wherein bishops were given jurisdiction over civil proceedings in which both parties were Christians and were granted other civic responsibilities and authority.[22] With these powers came the symbols of power commonly used by authority figures in the Roman Empire. These symbols took the form of titles, insignia such as special clothing, the honor of being accompanied in procession by incense and candles, and a special chair or throne at official proceedings, to name a few. The use of such symbols was not limited to civic proceedings but entered the liturgical gatherings of Christians as well. Klauser is careful to note that when the Roman Empire fell in the fifth century, these symbols were thoroughly transformed—spiritualized, as it were—and given such strong religious significance as to make them nearly unrecognizable from their civic, non-Christian origins. The use of these symbols throughout Church history, even now, is meant to point worshipers beyond the individual who bears such insignia to the holiness and apostolicity of the office he holds.[23]

These changes necessarily affected the average Christian's experience of worship. Such symbols of power would have added a beautiful nobility to the simple Christian service, and given its leaders an outward *gravitas* to match their inner dignity. But recall characteristic number 3 of early Christian worship, discussed above: It was done by all. Weak divisions existed between clergy and laity in the earliest Church, but these honors and insignia now in use by the leaders of the Church, who were also the leaders of liturgy, may have served to strengthen such divisions. (Other factors such as the formalization of clerical roles and differences in education level also played a role in the clergy-laity dynamic as history progressed). Indeed, partly because the leader of prayer represented Jesus as the head of the Church, it also affected the position of Christ in the perspective of worshipers. The transfer of Roman ideas and sentiments onto the Christian imagination, expressed in and out of the liturgy, gave heavy emphasis to Christ's universal dominion and authority over all nations, all peoples, all races. Christ was emphasized as the heavenly emperor of all creation. This is a wondrous, beautiful, and completely true image of who Christ is! But it easily overshadows the more human side of Christ, who was also a marginal Jew in Roman-occupied Palestine, executed by the state for challenging the religious establishment.

This emphasis, particularly in liturgy, on the transcendence over the immanence of God-in-Christ and the growing separation between clergy and laity was bound to follow Christian worship through the centuries to come. One of the most succinct ways to recognize these shifts is to trace them in the development of Church architecture. From Dura Europos (third century) to Sainte-Chapelle in France (thirteenth century), worship spaces became increasingly large, formal, grand, beautifully adorned, more rectangular with more height, more Roman and less Jewish, and most strikingly, the position of the faithful became estranged from the place of eucharistic action. Keep in mind the impetus for such estrangement was not to punish or put down the faithful but rather to give the Eucharist and the rituals of the Mass the formality and reverence they deserved. Eventually gates were used to give only certain ministers access to the sanctuary.

THE MASS MOVES WEST

The collapse of the Western Roman Empire, complete by the end of the fifth century, left a cultural and political void that the Christian Church—with its vast network of followers, radical sense of community, increasing internal organization, and ability to serve the social needs of the populace—rushed to fill. Historian Peter Brown notes the remarkable way in which Christianity went from a sect standing against, or at least at the margins of Roman society, to an organization ready to absorb the whole of Roman culture.[24]

With the collapse of the Western Empire, the Church's influence over the rulers of the East lost significance, and eventually a separation between the Churches of the East (centered in Constantinople) and West (centered in Rome) occurred. The Christian Eucharistic Rite of the Church of Rome, the core Word and Eucharist service prayed by the early Christians and augmented by Roman ceremonial and rhetoric, moved West into what is now France—and beyond—while continuing to develop and change. Frankish peoples had different, more fiery temperaments from the staid, unemotional Romans, and brought new, dramatic elements to the liturgy, with more verbose, florid language for expressing the rites. Eventually this meeting of cultures resulted in a hybridized form of the Mass that became predominant throughout the late Middle Ages:[25] the Franco-Roman liturgy.

It is useful to note that the language used in Mass had already changed twice by this time in history. In its first generations, Christian worship had been in Aramaic, the vernacular language of Jesus and his first disciples. Early in the first century it shifted to Greek, a more universal tongue, and remained the language of liturgy until the mid-third century, when Latin became normative.[26] Throughout its travels across the globe over the centuries to come, Latin would remain the operative language of the Roman Catholic Mass until 1963.

While the language of liturgy and the core cluster of rites remained stable throughout its long history, the Mass was to change dramatically from its earliest form. Picture a paper doll with no clothes on. Then picture adding one or two pieces of clothing—a dress, a hat, some shoes, a purse, etc.—for each child who plays with the doll. Then multiply the number of children who want to play with her by 100. What does the doll look like now? As the Mass moved West and entered new cultures, each of which both influenced and was influenced by the prayer of the Roman Church, the Mass gathered new elements, new rites, new devotional elaborations, even new physical accoutrement that were to turn it into a quite complicated act of worship. Cultural embellishments proliferated, ceremonial increased, and by the Middle Ages the Mass was heavily cluttered with ritual and difficult to recognize from its ancient expressions, so marked by simplicity and directness. Unlike the ancient liturgy, the medieval Mass would have been nearly impossible for the average person to comprehend without significant external interpretation.

In addition to these new layers of ritual, the Mass' language, architectural space, and music—while beautiful and reverent—exacerbated the people's inability to participate in their corporate worship during the medieval period. Latin had become a language understood only by the educated, so the words of the Mass were unintelligible to most in the assembly. And recall the shifts in architecture mentioned earlier: As the physical spaces where Mass was celebrated became more formal, more adorned, more grand, and with stricter separations between clergy and faithful, so too did the liturgy. Instead of the people's song, so integral to the people's prayer in the early Church, in the Frankish period choirs of professional singers—usually monks—thoroughly dominated the singing at Mass. (The intention here was good: The singing at Mass was regarded as too important to be left to amateurs; trained professionals would make the Church's worship as beautiful as possible.) And through the influence of the growing trend for priests to daily say a "private Mass" (that is, with no assembly), the presider not only stopped musically chanting those prayers that belonged to his office, but he often read them silently at public Masses as well.[27] The most regrettable outcome of these shifts was the clouding of the mystery that lies at the heart of the Mass: the gathered assembly's real participation in the paschal mystery of Christ. Though it was so clearly espoused in New Testament writings, so thoroughly embraced by the early Church, the paschal mystery was, by so many gradual shifts and well-intentioned adornments, more obscured than revealed by the celebration of Mass in the late Middle Ages.

I do not mean to paint a negative picture of the Church in the Middle Ages through my account of the Mass' trip through time. There are many good things to recognize about the medieval Church. As antiquity moved to the Middle Ages, the Church remained constant in a murky, violent world. It was both an influencer as well as a preserver of culture. The liturgy had a profound impact on the imaginations of the people of western Europe. Historian Eamon Duffy maintains the rhythms of the liturgical year were, for medieval people of all stripes, the rhythms of life itself.[28] The seven sacraments of the Church became the skeleton of the medieval social body. They held a significance and served functions in daily life that show our modern expressions of them to be mere shadows of their true meaning. For example, selection of godparents for your child from outside your relations was a way of extending the bonds of kinship beyond your family and reducing civil disputes, since godparents became legal as well as Church relatives, and family members were not permitted to sue one another. Especially in the early medieval period, penances were given in proportion and reparation for sins committed, so as to make right the wrong done to victims.[29] Infant baptism introduced a child as a full member of this thoroughly sacramental society, assuring him the right to a Christian education. While the Middle Ages were unruly and harsh, the sacramental structure of Christianity, as well as a host of Christian devotions and pious practices, were a force for stability and order: the much-needed societal glue.

We should also acknowledge the many liturgical developments of this long era that remain important to the Church's liturgy today, such as the composition and recording of many beloved prayers, still in use today, as well as the development of important liturgical books. The artful adornment of such books and objects used in the liturgy was also an important contribution of the medieval Church. The breathtaking sacred art and architecture of the medieval period stands as a monument to the ascendancy of the Roman Catholic Church in the Western medieval world. But viewed from a modern, pastoral perspective —especially one that emphasizes the spiritual engagement of the average Catholic in worship—the long period that led up to the Protestant Reformation was, for the Mass, a period of developmental decline.

THE PROTESTANT REFORMATION AND THE COUNTER-REFORMATION

One of the major theological trends that accompanied the Mass' trip from a small, informal, communal, participative meal to a grand, rubrical, and (for the assembly) passive event was an emphasis on the physical, literal transformation of the bread and wine into the Body and Blood of Christ. This literalism with regard to the Eucharist led to a strong sense of superstition surrounding the consecrated bread and wine; reports of hosts bleeding and sightings of Jesus in the Communion bread were fairly common. It also led to reception on the tongue (instead of in the hand) becoming normative; the hands of the faithful were too unholy to touch the host. Ultimately it helped lead to a decline in the faithful's reception of Communion altogether. As evidence of this decline, we know at the Fourth Lateran Council of 1215, the Church mandated that the faithful receive Communion at least once per year: during the Easter season.

If the Eucharist was so literally Jesus' flesh and blood to the average late-medieval Catholic, why would they cease to receive it? Wouldn't they want to receive it more often? Average Catholics, influenced by the superstitions of the day, would have been rather intimidated by contact with the actual flesh and blood of Christ. Perhaps you would be, too, if you'd heard the rumor about the host that actually bled at a nearby parish. Adding to the confusion, by the late Middle Ages there was a significant shift in perception from Jesus' oral-aural culture. While Jesus' culture favored the senses of hearing and speech as the preferred means of knowing and believing, people of the late Middle Ages preferred sight. Theirs was an ocular culture—with a bias for the eye—in which seeing is believing. This way of perceiving informs our modern Western culture, which is still largely sight-based. So for the late medieval person, simply seeing the host, elevated after the words of consecration, was sufficient to satisfy their devotion to Christ and perhaps a whole lot safer than actually consuming the host. In fact, the elevation of the host, instead of the reception of Communion by the faithful, became the most important moment in the Mass. Priests were given special stipends to prolong the elevation of host and chalice (even, reportedly, balancing the chalice on their heads![30]). Bells were rung to indicate this most important moment in the Mass to an assembly of people who, at the sound of these bells, would have interrupted their individual, private devotions to watch.

This objectification of the Eucharist—along with the many liturgical abuses, inconsistencies, and aberrations that had proliferated in the late medieval period—could not go forever unchecked. The voices of the Reformation that began to sound in the early sixteenth century were harbingers of needed change, but also, sadly, of the end of Christian unity and, with the severe truncation of the system of sacraments, an unfortunate disenchantment of popular culture.[31] Still, the reformers' emphases on faith over works, human freedom, and the importance and authority of Scripture were welcomed by many in this very mixed age: one of artistic beauty, sacramentality, eucharistic reverence and ecclesial influence, but also of corruption and liturgical disarray that had, in effect, marginalized the faithful.

The Church did not leave the abuses brought to light by the reformers unanswered. Liturgically speaking, the thrust of the Council of Trent, convened by the Church in 1545, was to "clean up" liturgical practice by cleaning up the books used in the celebration of the liturgy: consolidating some, revising all, and entrusting to the pope and his assistants the publication of one book, the *Missale Romanum* or *Roman Missal*, containing the readings, prayers and instructions or "rubrics" (from the Latin word *rubeo* for "red"; so named for the red print in which they appeared) for the celebration of Mass. This *Missal* was an ambitious project that answered a serious liturgical need and has brought great benefits to the Church ever since. The *Missal* was, with a few exceptions, to be binding on the Roman Catholic Church everywhere, and a Roman authority was installed to both interpret these rubrics and ensure that parishes everywhere conformed to them. Thus Klauser calls the ensuing epoch in the history of the Mass an age of rubricism, or strict adherence to rules governing liturgy.[32]

But it is difficult to ensure rigid uniformity in so vast a Church. *The Roman Missal* was not the answer to all the Church's problems, nor was it warmly or even obediently embraced everywhere. For one thing, certain churches, especially in France, had been given exceptions to continue celebrating a long-standing form of the Mass in their own regions. In France this was called the "Gallican" liturgy. And even in places where Rome had successfully implemented its new *Roman Missal*, the rubricism of its approach to reform, while rooting out some disturbing liturgical abuses, did not concretely address the lack of participation by the faithful in the mystery of the celebration. The Mass remained in Latin, a language unintelligible to the average worshiper. The priest, due to the overwhelming influence of the medieval practice of saying private Masses, stood at an altar affixed to the back wall of the sanctuary with his back to the assembly. He read the prayers of the Mass quietly if at all audibly, and responses were given only by those servers of the Mass who were permitted in the sanctuary. The people, for lack of engagement in the celebration at hand, took up personal devotions in the pews (such as the rosary, which had been popular since the Middle Ages), or sang devotional songs together while

Mass was going on. Klauser notes the faithful in this era were still receiving Communion but rarely, especially given the strict necessity for confessing one's sins before communicating.[33]

It's difficult to imagine the burden felt by Church authorities at this time as they attempted to prevent the Church of Jesus Christ from collapsing under the weight of both its internal and external problems. But the Holy Spirit guides the Church in good times and bad, and the Spirit undoubtedly led Church leaders to adopt a sort of "circle-the-wagons" approach to answering the reformers' grievances with the Church and its liturgy. This approach did much to end abuses, but further strategies would be needed—and thanks to the same Holy Spirit—would be provided to help bring the Mass closer in character to its apostolic roots.

THE LITURGICAL MOVEMENT AND THE EVE OF VATICAN II

In 1840, Catholic priest and scholar Dom Prosper Guéranger authored a book that would help to start a new movement in the Catholic Church and a new era in the history of the Mass. The book was on the Church's liturgical year: the rhythms of the paschal mystery that rise and fall over the course of each year in our ritual celebrations. Guéranger was French, and his country had been through a bloody and, for the Church, almost completely devastating revolution. The violently won equality and secularism of the new France had pushed Catholic thought and practice to the very margins of society. And where the Church was still viable in France, parish liturgies employed nationalistic "Gallican" traditions that were not in union with the Church of Rome. Much of Guéranger's scholarly work was intended to bring his country's celebration of liturgy in line with the Roman rubrics. Guéranger was a rigid Romanist, a romantic who idealized the Middle Ages (especially liturgical plainchant) and an ambitious reformer who set up an institute for liturgical study out of a disused and deteriorating Benedictine monastery in the French countryside. Solesmes Abbey became the center of a revival of the Benedictine order in Europe, and soon other monastery-institutes joined its ranks in France and beyond: Mont César, Maredsous, Maria Laach, and others. Guéranger is recognized as one of the founders of what is now known as the liturgical movement.

In its earliest stages the liturgical movement was academic. The romantic intellectual and artistic movement afoot in Europe at the time brought the study and admiration of past ages into vogue. Biblical and patristic (early Church) scholarship was on the rise, and archeological advances made them more fruitful, with discoveries of early biblical and liturgical manuscripts. This academic strain of the liturgical movement was extremely important and continued to fuel the movement throughout its lifespan.

But soon the pastoral implications of its scholarly findings became the liturgical movement's focus. This shift in the movement was aided by official papal sanction of its work in the form of a 1903 *motu proprio*, or special instruction by the pope, endorsing the study of liturgical music that Guéranger and his associates had undertaken. Significantly, the *motu proprio* named the "active participation" of the faithful as a value in liturgy, calling it the "indispensable source" of the Christian life.[34]

This idea of active participation in liturgy as the font of the true Christian spirit garnered attention from many scholars and pastors. It particularly interested one Benedictine priest named Lambert Beaduin. Beaduin had worked as a labor chaplain for French coal miners before entering Mont César to study the liturgy. His combined experiences must have influenced his ardent belief that liturgy ought not be reserved for the elite; Mass should be accessible to all the faithful.[35] He began teaching at St. Anselmo, the Benedictine Pontifical College in Rome, and there passed his ideas to a young, talented, American Benedictine named Virgil Michel (pronounced "Michael"). When Fr. Michel turned his prodigious talents to the study of the liturgy, he helped make a uniquely American contribution to the liturgical movement by articulating and promoting the liturgy as a model for a life of true justice in society. However, like democracy, this potential for the liturgy to model and effect justice in society hinged upon the people's active participation in it. You cannot have a true democracy if no one votes. In a similar way, the people do not enter into the mystical body of Christ if they remain silent spectators before the rites, occupying themselves with private devotions as the great paschal mystery unfolds before their unknowing eyes.

With these poignant revelations and assertions by folks like Beaduin and Michel, it became very obvious that the Mass, the official prayer of the Church, was in need of reform. However, it takes more than a movement—however influential—to make reforms in the Roman Catholic Church, especially to its liturgy. But the movement laid the groundwork for the reforms that were to come. In looking back on the liturgical movement, we can name the following values and principles that animated it for more than 100 years and that greatly influenced the age of liturgical reform it helped to usher in:

1. **Active participation** of the faithful in Mass through song, gesture, procession, listening, and responding or "dialogue";
2. **Scholarly examination** of the rites of Mass for continuity with the liturgy's apostolic roots;
3. **Catechesis** or Christian instruction of all the faithful on the meaning of the Mass, so as to enable more meaningful participation;

4. Reemphasis on the importance of **Scripture** to the liturgical celebration, as well as preaching on Scripture;

5. **Plainchant** (also known as "Gregorian chant") and congregational song as a means of engendering participative singing by the whole assembly together; and

6. The **paschal mystery** as the heart, the root, and the purpose of our liturgical praying.

By the mid-twentieth century, the liturgical movement had brought these principles to the forefront of thinking on the liturgy. Their achievement became the goal of a new age of reform for the Mass.

DISCUSSION QUESTIONS

1. *Read Luke 24:13-25 (the Emmaus story), the earliest model of Christian worship. In what ways does it model the Mass? What is most interesting to you about this story?*

2. *What did Sunday mean to the earliest Christians? What does it mean to Christians today?*

3. *The earliest Christians expected the Second Coming of Jesus any day. How would your life be different if you shared this expectation?*

4. *Of the seven characteristics of early Christian worship mentioned in the chapter, which one surprised or interested you the most? Why?*

5. *In what ways did the emperor Constantine's conversion change Christian worship?*

6. *What factors in the development of Christian worship throughout the Middle Ages caused the faithful's active participation in the Mass to diminish? Did these developments surprise you? Why or why not?*

7. *What was the liturgical movement, and how did it pave the way for the liturgical reform of the Second Vatican Council?*

CHAPTER 3

What It's All About: Celebration and Participation in the Paschal Mystery

A t this point you may be feeling bogged down in the history of the Mass. Even those who enjoy history often feel somewhat despondent after reading accounts of the celebration of Mass becoming so distant from the faithful throughout time. But as I said in the last chapter, the Holy Spirit, ever our guide, inspired the Church's scholars and leaders to usher in a new era. The liturgical movement of the nineteenth and twentieth centuries brought the people's participation in Mass—and more specifically their celebration and participation in the paschal mystery—back to the forefront of thinking on liturgy.

SACROSANCTUM CONCILIUM AND THE SPIRIT OF VATICAN II

In 1959, when the newly elected Pope John XXIII called a worldwide Church council to undertake the first reform of canon law since the Council of Trent in 1545, it was safe to assume the reform of the liturgy would play an important role. Before the Second Vatican Council opened, a preparatory committee was formed to assess and articulate needs to be addressed at the council. The council preparatory committee then invited the bishops of the world to send ideas for subjects the council should take in hand. Almost one-fourth of the resultant requests had to do with the liturgy, especially in areas of the world considered "mission territory," where many non-Catholics and non-Christians lived. There was urgent need for a reform of the rites of the Church in order to make them more accessible to those people with whom the Church sought to share the Gospel message. But even in places like Europe and the United States, where Catholicism was well-established, there remained grave concerns about the Tridentine Mass' inability to engage Catholics in their faith and its implications for their daily living. Amid such concerns and a worldwide chorus of cries for liturgical reform, the Second Vatican Council opened in 1962.

The August-September 1963 edition of the American academic journal on liturgy called *Worship*, founded in 1926 by Fr. Virgil Michel as a voice for the liturgical movement in America, contains an excerpt of a lecture by Professor Joseph Ratzinger titled "The First Session." A German diocesan priest and scholar, Professor Ratzinger had attended the council in the role of *peritus* (Latin for "expert"), to provide theological expertise at the request of a German cardinal. In his *Worship* piece, Professor Ratzinger, now known to Catholics all over the world as Emeritus Pope Benedict XVI, gave his impressions of the opening session of the Second Vatican Council and the debate over the principles of liturgy to be adopted by the council. The future Holy Father began by remarking on the opening ceremonies of the council, which seemed burdensome in their length and complexity and failed to encourage the participation of the 2,500 bishops of the world in attendance. Professor Ratzinger remarked that this sad lack of engagement seemed a symptom of the ailing current state of the liturgy and needed to be remedied by the council.[36]

Professor Ratzinger went on to delineate the basic aims and tendencies of the proposed document on liturgy, which was to ground the reform of the liturgy in the age to come and the bishops' discussions thereof. First, he said, the proposed document emphasizes a return to the origins of the liturgy and a removal of many layers of ritual that had shrouded the core of what Mass seeks to convey: the paschal mystery. This meant softening the ritual stiffness Fr. Ratzinger felt impeded the Mass' appeal and significance for modern worshipers. The document emphasized the public, communal celebration of the Mass over private Masses, which in turn would highlight the dialogic nature of the Mass: Mass as dialogue between priest (who represents Christ) and people (the Church). Next, reported Fr. Ratzinger, the proclamation of Scripture is to play a more significant role in liturgy, and the council was to make an emphatic recommendation of the homily on Sundays and holy days of obligation. (Until this time homilies were not always included in Mass and often addressed issues of faith and morality instead of breaking open the Scriptures of the day.) The council also seemed to adopt the liturgical movement's special concern for active participation, and Fr. Ratzinger remarked that one could see this concern reflected in the proposed document's permission for the faithful to receive Communion under both bread and wine; to this point, only the bread had been available to the assembly in Mass.

According to Fr. Ratzinger, two further topics garnered discussion by the bishops of the world on the proposed document on liturgy: liturgical governance and language. First the council proposed to decentralize liturgical control. The Council of Trent in 1545 had put the decision-making powers about liturgy exclusively into Roman hands, but the Second Vatican Council sought to shift this power, giving conferences of bishops in various regions around the world the authority to legislate certain liturgical matters for the people they served. This was an important pastoral decision, intended to allow the talents and cultures of people all over the world to contribute to the Mass, creating truly "catholic"—that is to say universal—worship. Though this shifting of power seemed to Professor Ratzinger an important ecclesial change, he reports the more lengthy and lively debate on the liturgy during the first session was over language. Latin had been the language of the Roman Catholic Mass since the fourth century. The Catholic Church does not make change casually in any matter and certainly not to a tradition so ancient as the language of the liturgy. But, said those pushing for change, why bother to reform the liturgy—the simplification of rites, the renewal of the liturgical dialogues, the re-emphasis on Scripture, the push for the assembly's participation, and all the rest—if the Mass was still to be celebrated in a language that was not merely foreign to the assembly but archaic and out of common use? The council sought to expand the use of the vernacular in the liturgy, and after much debate, moved forward in this direction. Professor Ratzinger reports that despite the lively debate on this and other topics, when it came time for the bishops to vote, the proposed principles behind the forthcoming document on liturgy to be authored by Vatican Council II were overwhelming accepted.

The resulting document, *Sacrosanctum Concilium* or the Constitution on the Sacred Liturgy (hereinafter CSL), was the first of sixteen documents published by the council on topics ranging from the identity of the Catholic Church to the Church's relationship with the modern world, from ecumenism to social communication, from the education of priests to the education of children. Following upon that ancient wisdom discussed in chapter 1 of this book, which claims "the law of praying is the law of believing," the CSL was the first of Vatican II's canon of documents and set the tone for the rest of the council's work. The paschal mystery, placed by the CSL firmly at the center of the Church's celebrations of the Mass, was then placed by the council's other documents at the center of the Church's sacramental theology and thinking about the person of Christ (or Christology). The image of the mystical body of Christ, so central to the CSL's understanding of the gathered assembly at prayer, became the new-old ecclesiology of the Vatican II Church.

The CSL put forth not specific rubrics or detailed instructions on how to change the way we celebrate the Mass, but gave guiding principles for reform and is therefore often called the "blueprint" for liturgical reform. (Blueprints only show you the outline of a structure: where walls, doors, and stairs will be, but not furniture and decorations.) I have also heard the CSL called the "Magna Carta" of modern liturgy; this says much about the weight of the CSL's authority over our liturgical practice, which is difficult to overestimate. It is important to recognize that while the CSL can be viewed as a progressive document that embraced change, its ratification by the bishops of the world was not controversial. Professor Ratzinger reported that the preliminary discussion of the CSL's proposed content ended in a lopsidedly affirmative vote among the bishops; when it came time for a vote on the document itself, the bishops were almost unanimously in favor of its acceptance. The final vote by the bishops of the world ratifying the Constitution on the Sacred Liturgy was 2,147 to four.[37]

This overwhelming agreement among the bishops is evidence that the time was ripe for the reform of the Mass, and that the liturgical movement, in 100 or so years of scholarship and education toward reform, had reached its peak. Now, guided by the principles of the CSL, it was time to move on to the hard work of real reform. In the CSL, those liturgical scholars and experts entrusted with this delicate work had a worthy manifesto. We will refer to the content of the CSL (which is available in its full form in English on the Vatican's website: vatican.va) throughout the rest of this book as we discuss the Mass, but for now let's scan the document to see, in brief, how it informs our modern liturgy.

The first section of the CSL addresses the nature of the liturgy and its essential role in the life of the Church. The central phrase in this section is "paschal mystery": Christ's redeeming work of life, death, and resurrection, but also the perpetuation of that work in the sacramental celebrations of Christ's body, the Church. In these celebrations, asserts the CSL, Christ is truly present, and the four modes of his presence in the liturgy are named: in the presiding minister, the gathered assembly, the Word, and the consecrated bread and wine, or Communion. Here the CSL calls the liturgy "the summit toward which the activity of the Church is directed; at the same time it is the font from which all her power flows."[38] This potent idea about the nature of the liturgy in relationship to the Church's power and activity is often shortened to "liturgy is the source and summit" and is perhaps the most well-known and influential idea about liturgy from the CSL. It both affirms and furthers the assertions of liturgical movement heroes such as Lambert Beaduin and Virgil Michel, who had drawn bold connections between liturgy and the life of Christians in the world. Finally, this first section concludes with some new expectations for both priests and people. The people are admonished to come to liturgy with proper dispositions for a thoughtful experience of worship: a conscious encounter with Christ and his Church. For priests, the CSL ends the Tridentine epoch of rubricism; "something more is required," it says, "than the mere observation of the laws governing valid and licit [lawful] celebration."[39] It is now a pastor's duty not only to read the prayers and follow the rubrics but also to ensure the faithful are engaged and enriched by the celebration of the Mass.

The next section of the CSL continues this theme of engagement in liturgy by focusing on the importance of liturgical instruction for all Catholics as a means of fostering active participation. Each Christian, it says, because of baptism in Christ, has both the right *and* the *obligation* to participate fully in the Mass. The constitution goes so far as to say, "Mother Church earnestly desires that all the faithful should be led to that fully conscious, and active participation in liturgical celebrations which is demanded by the very nature of the liturgy."[40] It then recommends liturgical education for all members of the Catholic Church so as to make this full participation in Mass possible.

Next, the CSL puts forth guidelines for the reform of the liturgy consistent with those Professor Ratzinger detailed in his *Worship* article: a return to origins including simplification of rites, a re-emphasis on the importance of Scripture and homilies and on the public, communal nature of Mass, and the fostering of active participation of all in liturgy. Finally, the CSL expands the use of the people's vernacular language, Communion under both bread and wine, and encourages the talents and customs of various races of peoples in the Roman Catholic Mass, "so long as they harmonize with its true and authentic spirit."[41] This section shifts liturgical decision-making to regional bishops and recommends the establishment of commissions of experts to help guide the local bishop in matters of liturgy. Subsequent sections of the CSL apply its vision for liturgy to the celebrations of sacraments such as baptism and marriage, to the liturgical year, sacred music, sacred art and furnishings, and to the praying of the Divine Office.

Subsequent documents on liturgy, issued by both the Vatican and regional conferences of bishops, followed the CSL and helped flesh out the CSL's more general directives. The most important of these documents was *The General Instruction of The Roman Missal* (*GIRM*) in 1974. This document helped (and, in revised form, still helps) interpret the new *Order of Mass* and *The Roman Missal* released in the late 1960s at the prompting of the CSL. Documents were also issued by both the Vatican and the U.S. Catholic bishops on the subject of liturgical music, and these also furthered the CSL's vision for paschal mystery-centered liturgy that fosters the full, active, conscious participation of the people.

WHAT IT'S ABOUT: CELEBRATION, PARTICIPATION, PASCHAL MYSTERY

Are you getting tired of the word "participation" yet? It certainly became a buzz word with regard to liturgy, starting with the liturgical movement in the late 1800s. The CSL's pronouncement that full, conscious, and active participation by the faithful in Mass "is demanded by the very nature of the liturgy"[42] certainly gave the phrase force. But why such emphasis on participation by the faithful? Surely the sacrament of Eucharist, and the Church which has celebrated it for thousands of years, are effective dispensers of grace whether or not the people sing, speak, gesticulate, and process during Mass...right? Right. And yet, as the CSL states, the proper disposition of the faithful who come to worship—their cooperation and participation with the profound graces offered by the celebration—is necessary "in order that the liturgy may be able to produce its *full* effects."[43] Yes, the liturgy is effective whether or not we participate fully, but its *full* effectiveness is our new goal, laid out for us by the Vatican II reforms.

And what is to be gained from such fullness in our liturgical experience? Teaching and learning the dialogues, gestures, music, and movements that engender the assembly's participation is hard work! Even harder work is that of growing in consciousness, both as individuals and as a community of believers, of what these symbolic sensory engagements mean. What justifies all this extra effort on the part of Catholics since Vatican II?

I have two words for you: **paschal mystery**. In these two words is hidden a reality so profound, so cosmic, so essential to what it means—and what it could mean—to be human, that we'll spend the rest of the chapter unpacking it. Indeed, we'll spend the rest of the book doing so. We could spend the rest of our lives unpacking it and we'd still be left in awe of its inscrutability! Fortunately, we who share in this paschal mystery know we are on pilgrimage in this life, and the journey is as important as the destination. So let's get started, shall we?

What do we mean when we say "paschal mystery?" Certain of you may have your hands in the air already. Every time I give a presentation on the paschal mystery, at least one well-informed person is sure he or she knows the "answer" to this question: "the paschal mystery is the life, passion, death, and resurrection of Jesus!" Congratulations, that is correct! It is, however, not the *whole* answer to the question. One could also correctly answer this question by saying "the paschal mystery is what every Catholic liturgy celebrates!" or "the paschal mystery designates the essential aspects of Christian redemption!" or "the paschal mystery is an abbreviation for the Easter mysteries!"[44] But even if someone offered each of these fine answers in quick succession, there would still be much, much more to say. This is because all of these answers could be filed under "what happened with Jesus." Yes, the paschal mystery, at its core, has to do with the redemptive work of Christ. But as big a story as the events in the life of Jesus comprise, they only made sense in the Jewish imaginations of the first Christians as part of a much larger story: the story of the Hebrew people's salvation by God. To get the most meaning out of the phrase "paschal mystery," we have to understand it in the context of the whole history of salvation, including the present, and even the end times yet to come. To try to understand the paschal mystery as something more than "what happened with Jesus," let's take a look at each of its component words: "paschal" and "mystery."

"Paschal"

The word "paschal" may ring a bell. It comes from the Greek form of an older Hebrew word, *pesach*, which referred to the ancient Jewish celebration of the Passover, or the annual commemoration of Israel's escape from slavery in Egypt. These are the events recounted in the first part of the Book of Exodus, a very exciting, suspenseful section of Scripture. In the story,

God's people the Hebrews have become slaves to the Egyptian Pharaoh and are not permitted to leave their labors to worship God in the desert, as their religion requires. They cry out to God, and he hears their cry and answers by sending a representative to lead them to freedom: Moses. Moses is an unlikely hero. Having escaped Pharaoh's campaign to kill Jewish boys as a baby through the ingenuity of his mother, he was raised as a prince in the royal household. But his impetuousness in killing an Egyptian for beating a Jew one day causes Moses to flee to the desert, where he takes up with a Jewish family and becomes a shepherd. One day as he tends his father-in-law's flocks, Moses sees a wondrous sight: a manifestation of God as a bush on fire yet unconsumed by the flames. God calls Moses to free the Hebrews from bondage and lead them to a new land: a land of freedom and prosperity. Although Moses is full of doubt and insecurity, he agrees to act for God, and God empowers him to go to Pharaoh with God's demands.

However, Pharaoh's heart is hardened to Moses' commands, and so God sends a series of ten plagues upon the Egyptians. Rivers run with blood, there are pests, disease, severe weather, even total darkness for three days, but none convince Pharaoh to liberate his free labor force, the Hebrews. The final, tenth plague, however, is one Pharaoh cannot withstand: death to the firstborn of every household in Egypt. God gives Moses careful instructions so that his own people are spared this terrible loss. Hebrew households are to slaughter an unblemished lamb and smear its blood across the top of their doorway to signal the Lord to pass over (hence, "Passover") their home, leaving their firstborns unharmed. And so it happens. Pharaoh, in his grief, not only allows but orders Moses and the Hebrews to depart, asking for a blessing on himself from their powerful God.

So Moses and the Israelites flee Egypt into the wilderness, with God leading them by day as a pillar of cloud and by night as a pillar of fire. But Pharaoh's heart is hardened once more, and he sends an army after the Hebrews to bring them back into his service. Pursued by the Egyptians with the Red Sea before them, Moses and the people are trapped. But the Lord instructs Moses to stretch out his staff, splitting the sea in two. In the story's most iconic moment, the people of God cross to safety on dry land with the waters of the sea like great walls on either side. But Pharaoh's pursuing army is drowned by the waters of the sea when, at Moses' command, they return to their normal depth. Standing in safety on the opposite shore, the Israelites come to fully believe in the Lord and in his servant Moses, and they sing a song of praise to their triumphant hero-God.

What an exciting story! But what does it have to do with Jesus and his paschal mystery? To answer this question, we have to look closer at the story and its significance. Why is this story so important to the Jewish people, even today? What does the story tell us about humans, God, and their relationship?

Let's start with God. In this story, God hears the prayers of his people and answers them. God is the hero of this story. He is an actor in human history and affairs and intervenes to create outcomes pleasing to himself. And—make no mistake—in Exodus, God wants to be worshiped by his people. In chapter 1 of this book, we discussed the nature of this desire of God: not as an egotistical need for attention but as a desire for closeness, for "quality time" with his people the Hebrews. In Exodus, God gives his name to Moses as "I Am" and appears in mysterious visions of flame to Moses and the people. God is not like us; he is fraught with mystery, with enigmatic energy, and the steadfastness of his existence cannot be grasped by our human imaginations. We can't put a "handle" on this God; even his name is elusive. Indeed one of the most mysterious aspects to the story is God's continual hardening of Pharaoh's heart. The story specifies that Pharaoh doesn't just keep changing his mind, but rather God *makes* Pharaoh refuse to let the Hebrews go for so long, and God *changes* Pharaoh's mind about letting them go in the end, causing the destruction of Pharaoh's army. Is God cruel, controlling, and sadistic? The text only implies what God wishes the Egyptian (and Hebrew) people to know: that *God* is God, and Pharaoh is *not* God.

Now let's look at Moses in the story. First we can see that, although God draws Moses out to be his representative to Pharaoh, in the story world Moses also represents humanity, with its flaws and sinfulness. Moses is in exile himself as a Jew living as an Egyptian, and the crime that causes him to flee Egypt shows both his rash violence and his tendency for compassion on those who are unfairly treated. When God appears before him in the burning bush and calls him into service, Moses' disinclination to obey God is almost embarrassing, and yet he carries out God's commands, coming into his God-given power as the story progresses. Moses, in his representation of humanity, recalls the first human—Adam from the Book of Genesis—and yet redeems this image of the sinful first man through his (albeit reluctant) obedience to God. Further, Moses is blamed and mistreated by the people he is sent to lead, who exclaim, when cornered by the pursuing army, "What have you done to us, bringing us out of Egypt?" (Exodus 14:11). But again and again, Moses overcomes the doubts of the people, his own insecurities, and even his sinfulness to lead God's people to freedom.

The significance of this story in the history of the Jewish people cannot be overestimated. The story profoundly shaped their ritual practices as the annual commemoration of the Passover surpassed all other feasts in importance. The story also shaped their relationship with God and their spiritual expectations. God intervenes in human history in a radical way in Exodus, rescuing them from their enemies and showing a clear partiality for his own people.

Although the Hebrews' freedom from slavery was achieved in such a heroic and triumphant way, what followed in their history was less glorious. They wandered for forty years, looking for the land God had promised them. They lived hard in the desert, grumbled against the Lord despite his providing food to sustain them, and even fell into the worship of other gods. When they finally found their "Promised Land," it was occupied! But the story of their liberation from Egypt taught them to hope: for freedom, for prosperity, for a passage from darkness to light, from death to new life. To this Passover people, the deep, dark waters of death may just be the waters of rebirth to a new, better life. In his letter titled *Sacramentum Caritatis* on the subject of the Eucharist, Pope Benedict XVI speaks eloquently of the hope sustained in the Jewish people by their celebrations of the Passover meal:

> This ritual meal...was a remembrance of the past, but at the same time a prophetic remembrance, *the proclamation of a deliverance yet to come*...their earlier liberation was not definitive, for their history continued to be marked by slavery and sin. The remembrance of their ancient liberation thus expanded to the invocation and expectation of *a yet more profound, radical, universal and definitive salvation*.[45]

Above all, the story of the Passover taught the Jewish people to hope that someday a new Moses would come, bringing the final liberation from the continued frailty of their human condition. In the story of the Exodus and its annual commemoration at Passover, we see the stirrings of hope for the Messiah.

"MYSTERY"

As we move to the word "mystery" in the all-important two-word phrase "paschal mystery," a word of caution is necessary. We modern, Western people tend to hear the word "mystery" in a fairly specific way, and that way differs from the scriptural sense of the word. We think of Sherlock Holmes, the books of

Agatha Christie and John Grisham, or crime shows like *CSI: Crime Scene Investigation* and *Cold Case Files*. These stories, virtually without exception, end when the mystery is solved. The main characters always riddle it out through their ingenuity and effort. Murder and crime mysteries have become so popular in the last 100 or so years because we modern people feel a deep sense of satisfaction in solving a mystery, in working out a puzzle, in eliminating the unknown. "Mystery," in this sense, is something to be solved: a conundrum we humans will work out if we have enough time or talent.

If we're going to eke as much meaning as possible from the phrase "paschal mystery," it would be best to try to put aside this modern understanding of the word "mystery." When we use "mystery" in the phrase "paschal mystery," it does not imply some puzzle we humans can and will solve, nor does it indicate something that cannot be understood because it is unintelligible. "Mystery" in the Christian, scriptural sense says something of the vastness and inscrutability of the life of God. It is best understood as encompassing the idea of this life of God as Trinity, affirming yet not explaining the impenetrable reality of the three persons of the Godhead: Father, Son, and Holy Spirit.

In the first place, this Trinitarian meaning of "mystery" in "paschal mystery" means the mystery of God (that is, God the Father, the first person of the Holy Trinity). The mystery of God refers to God's plan of salvation for us and for all the world, which is known and understood by God alone. What's that? No one told you there was a plan for your salvation? Perhaps no one has put it in those terms, but you do know of this plan. You have heard about it as it has unfolded (thus far) in the pages of Scripture. God's plan for our salvation began not with Jesus, not with the saving of the Hebrews from slavery in the Exodus, not even with the Flood. God's plan for our salvation began at creation, and the first words of the Bible tell of its genesis "in the beginning." Our salvation, that is our total union with him and the fullness of the life he desires for us, has concerned God from the very beginning. God *made* us in order to *save* us. And did this plan end with Jesus Christ's redemption of the world by his cross and resurrection? Not hardly. God's plan will end on that day when Christ returns to earth to bring all of us home to God: at the Second Coming. So when you're trying to remember what we mean when we say "the mystery of God," just remember it is God's plan of salvation for us and all the world that begins at the beginning of the Bible in the Book of Genesis and ends at the end of the Bible with the events foretold in the Book of Revelation.

Lest you feel too frustrated by such a vast, unknowable plan for the world's salvation, I have some good news (or should I say Good News?) for you. The mystery of God, though it is known and understood only by God, can and has been revealed to us in the person of Jesus Christ. The second sense of the word "mystery" in "paschal mystery" refers to this mystery of Christ, the Son, the second member of the Holy Trinity. In this second sense of the word "mystery," the two words of the phrase "paschal mystery" come together. In Jesus, the hopes of the Jewish people are fulfilled. Christ is the new and improved Moses (as well as the new Adam), who liberates humans from their mortality, not by making them deathless like gods but by destroying the power of death to separate them from God, even from one another.

And how did Christ do this? How did he affect the redemption of the human race, leading us out of the slavery and exile of our mortality and sinfulness? By obedience to the Father. Christ, in his complete obedience, utterly transcends his forerunner Moses. The epistle proclaimed at Mass on Palm Sunday each year tells of Christ's obedience best:

> Christ Jesus, though he was in the form of God,
>> did not regard equality with God
>> as something to be grasped.

> Rather, he emptied himself,
>> taking the form of a slave,
>> coming in human likeness;
>> and found human in appearance,
>> he humbled himself,
>> becoming obedient to death,
>> even death on a cross.
>
> Because of this, God greatly exalted him
>> and bestowed on him the name
>> that is above every name,
>> that at the name of Jesus
>> every knee should bend,
>> of those in heaven and on earth and under the earth,
>> and every tongue confess that
>> Jesus Christ is Lord,
>> to the glory of God the Father (Philippians 2:6–11).

Jesus' fragility and vulnerability recalled, in the religious imaginations of his first disciples, that innocent, perfect Passover lamb who was sacrificed by the people. The blood of this lamb was an emblem of their chosen-ness by God and a sign for God to spare them from death. Thus Jesus is both the "new Moses" and also the "Lamb of God." Even by the time John's Gospel is recorded around AD 120, Jesus' followers had worked out this paschal connection. When we first meet Jesus in John's Gospel he is called "the Lamb of God, who takes away the sin of the world" (1:29b). And in John's Gospel, the events of the Last Supper and crucifixion occur one day earlier than in the other Gospels. In Matthew, Mark, and Luke, Jesus' Last Supper is a Passover meal. In John it occurs the night *before* Passover, putting the preparations for Passover (which would have included the slaughtering of a lamb) during the exact time of Jesus' crucifixion. John likely ordered the events this way, not because those other Gospels had it wrong, but because he wanted his telling of the Good News to emphasize this image of Christ as the paschal lamb. It is a powerful image, and there is no wonder John's Gospel, though different, found a place in the New Testament. Indeed John's Christology became the most influential to the Church's understanding, as expressed in its liturgies, of the redemptive work of Christ in the context of God's plan for our salvation.

To refer again to the 2005 papal encyclical *Sacramentum Caritatis*, Pope Benedict XVI says the love that Christ has and teaches by his paschal mystery is "love in its most radical form. In the Paschal Mystery, our deliverance from evil and death has taken place."[46] Indeed the love Christ showed throughout his ministry was often baffling to his disciples—even those, like Peter, who were closest to him didn't always "get" Jesus' teachings and example of loving self-sacrifice. Earlier I said John's account of the Last Supper is not a Passover meal; the meal itself is completely upstaged by a strange action by Jesus. "During supper," it says, Jesus rises and strips off his outer garment. (I once heard a scholar say that he probably didn't have an inner garment, since he was relatively poor, and thus the passage indicates Jesus' literal nakedness and complete vulnerability before his disciples.) Then he kneels to wash the feet of each disciple. In John's Gospel, this radical act of personal service takes the place of the eucharistic meal described in the other Gospels and helps us understand the meal as a measure for our lives: lives of radical love and humble service. This is how sin and death are destroyed: by Christ's showing the world, through the Eucharist of his Body and Blood, that love is stronger than death. This is the heart of the paschal mystery: dying to self, rising to new life in Christ.

The loving self-sacrifice of the Lamb of God takes away the sin of the world, freeing humanity from slavery to sin and death. But do not forget that the sacrificial lamb in the story of the Passover of the Jews was also meant as food for their journey to freedom. And so, in the mystery of the Church, the third aspect of the word "mystery" in "paschal mystery," Christ sustains his people on their journey homeward through real food and drink in his most holy sacrament of the Eucharist. This third and final aspect of "mystery" refers to the ritual and sacramental life shared by the members of the Church as one body in Christ. If you have been following my Trinitarian explanation of "mystery" closely, you might wonder why the third aspect of "mystery" is not the mystery of the *Holy Spirit*, and rightly so. But recall the Holy Spirit is said to have founded the Church on earth, bringing it to birth at Pentecost. Though the Holy Spirit may have many "homes" on earth, in the Catholic tradition the Church is its privileged dwelling place among us.

Through the Church, and especially through her celebrations of the Mass, the paschal mystery is revealed, and we who celebrate are invited into the story. We answer this invitation first by showing up to Mass, then by our full, active, conscious participation in the celebration through gesture, posture, prayer, procession, and song. But the most important way in which we participate in the paschal mystery to which Christ invites us is through partaking in the Lord's Supper: the Body and Blood of Christ at Communion. As you know, Catholics believe the bread and wine, though unchanged in their properties (they still look, smell, taste like bread and wine), become in their essence or "substance" the true Body and Blood of Christ. This "transubstantiation," as we call it, causes Catholics to observe special practices in our handling, distribution, and presence before the sacred species that other Christians do not. While such practices may seem strange, like the care we take with crumbs of the host or the special way we clean the holy vessels used at Communion, they are all reminders of the Real Presence of Christ with us in the Eucharist.

What's more, such practices remind us of the transformation that takes place within ourselves when we eat of his flesh and drink of his blood—we become Christ! St. Augustine's famous

Sermon 272 eloquently explains this greatest mystery of the Church; the heart of his message is often shortened to "receive what you are; become what you receive." Our hearts were made to be like Christ's, but sin keeps us from true communion with God. In the Eucharist, we are called back to this communion through the loving self-sacrifice of God's Son, Jesus. What we offer at the table is our very selves; what we receive is ourselves made new in Christ.

Perhaps most importantly, the mystery of the Church, whose members partake in and become the body of Christ, is the vehicle by which Christ's paschal mystery, Christ's perpetual dying and rising, continues to be revealed in the world. The Constitution on the Sacred Liturgy says this is the reason Christ instituted the Eucharist in the first place: "in order to perpetuate the sacrifice of the Cross throughout the centuries until He should come again, and so to entrust to His beloved spouse, the Church, a memorial of His death and resurrection: a sacrament of love, a sign of unity, a bond of charity, a paschal banquet...."[47] St. Teresa of Ávila captured the same reality more simply. Christ, she said, has no body on earth now but ours. Ours are his hands and feet now, and our eyes look with his compassion on the world. If we are unwilling to enter into his paschal mystery of dying to self and rising to new life—to allow our hands to become his own—the work of Christ cannot continue. And as the Constitution on the Sacred Liturgy tells us, the liturgy is the "source and summit" of this life of Christ, so our doing the work of Christ both begins and culminates with our celebrations of Mass. This work is never finished; the many processions in the Mass remind us we are a pilgrim people. We will only arrive at the kingdom we are building in the end of time, when Christ himself brings us through the gates. In the meantime, we work. This is the mystery of the Church.

THE PASCHAL MYSTERY AND LITURGICAL TIME

The paschal mystery of Christ becomes, through these celebrations, much more than a historical moment in time we wish to remember, though it is that. It also becomes a present reality that defines us and an eternal hope to which we hold fast. The structure and rhythm of liturgical time makes this past-present-future-ness of our paschal mystery celebrations more clear.

Our time as a Church is organized around two poles of theological importance: the Incarnation of Christ at Christmas and the resurrection of Christ at Easter. The Church's year begins around the end of November in Advent, the season that prepares for and awaits the birth of Christ. The first part of Advent reminds us of the darkness in the world and our longing for the Second Coming of Christ, who will dispel all evil in the end. The latter part of Advent focuses on preparing our hearts to receive Christ in his first coming at Christmas. The Christmas season celebrates this coming, this Incarnation: God brought to birth among us, taking up our human frailty as his own. Through the Scriptures, prayers, and hymns of Mass, the darkness of Advent gives way to the light of Christmas.

A period of ordinary time (where weeks are numbered with ordinal numbers like "First" and "Fifth," hence the name) follows Christmas, and then another important preparatory season begins: Lent. Lent was originally a time of final preparation for those joining the Church through baptism at Easter. Later it became a penitential period, and now both characteristics define Lent: repentance for sin and preparation to receive or renew our baptism at Easter. We fast in Lent, dying to our physical desires, both as a means of penance and as a means of emptying ourselves to make room for the fullness of our spiritual joy at Easter. For there is no more joyful, wondrous—and short!—season as the season of Triduum. The Great Paschal Triduum is a complex of rites that make up one, three-day-long celebration of the paschal mystery: Holy Thursday of the Lord's Supper (on Thursday evening), Good Friday of the Lord's passion, the Vigil of the Lord's Resurrection on Holy Saturday, and Easter Sunday. (One of my students appropriately nicknamed the Triduum "Paschalpalooza.") The Triduum is followed by a fifty-day season of unbounded joy, hope, and paschal mystery goodness. Why fifty days? Because fifty is ten more than the forty days of Lent, and in the Catholic tradition, joy is stronger than sorrow, and love is stronger than death.

The Easter season ends with the great feast of Pentecost, a word that literally means "fifty" and that celebrates the sending of the Holy Spirit to the apostles. Then come the important theological feasts of Holy Trinity and Corpus Christi, which begin a long stretch of ordinary time wherein the ministry and teachings of Jesus are broken open and celebrated. As winter approaches in many places and the last leaves fall from the trees, we near the final feast of the year: the Solemnity of Our Lord Jesus Christ the King. The readings and prayers of Mass turn our hearts again to the end of time and to our longing for Christ to come in glory as both judge and liberator of our world. As the year dies and Advent comes again, the Church sings songs of hope and patient waiting for "ever more perfect union with God and with each other, so that finally God may be all in all." [48]

THE PASCHAL MYSTERY AND THE MINISTERS OF THE MASS

Let's wrap up this chapter by taking a brief look at how the paschal mystery enlivens the various ministries of the Mass. How do those with special roles in the Mass fulfill their ministries so as to manifest the dying and rising of Christ?

The presider has the principal role in the celebration of Mass. His life of sacrifice as an ordained minister, together with any assisting deacons, helps him approach his liturgical ministry with a Christ-like attitude of radical, service-oriented love. First and foremost he prays both on behalf of the gathered assembly and also with them. Despite his many responsibilities, he always takes part in the praying and singing of the assembly with enthusiasm. His bearing in liturgy is never showy or ostentatious, but humble and dignified, as befits his duty to "convey to the faithful the living presence of Christ." [49] It is not the priest's duty to reinvent the liturgy or interpret it for the people through additions or changes but rather to faithfully and humbly offer the sacrifice, according to the liturgical tradition that has been entrusted to him in the place of Christ and on behalf of his Church. At the same time, he is entrusted with the leadership of the team of people who prepare the liturgy, from music ministers to servers. He must collaborate with others while upholding a clear vision and high standards for the liturgy. His own careful preparation of the rites, homily, and prayers that belong to his office are essential and will bear the fruit of grace, beauty, and insight to the community. The presider and assisting deacons, called to lead effectively yet with honest humility, have perhaps the most challenging and certainly the most crucial roles in helping break open the paschal mystery in the Mass.

The ministers of music also have abundant opportunities for showing and living the paschal mystery in their duties at Mass. They must be competent and talented musicians yet not performers; their primary responsibility is to facilitate and encourage the assembly's singing. They choose the music for Mass not based on personal preferences for particular styles, songs, or hymns, but based on careful, prayerful discernment of which music best helps the gathered assembly enter into the paschal mystery through the more specific themes brought to light in the readings, prayers, season, or occasion. This is no easy task! For example, most professional liturgical musicians I know are really, *really* tired of the song "On Eagle's Wings" by J. Michael Joncas. It's a very nice song, just overused, and many musicians I know would rather leave it on the proverbial shelf in favor of something fresher or in a different style. But in most places in the U.S., "On Eagle's Wings" will generate such strong participation by the assembly, and its lyrical themes are so ready for the occasion, the music minister would usually be wise to use it for a funeral, especially if it is requested. They may not like playing it themselves, but their job is to die to their own desires in order to best serve the assembly's prayer. In this sense, they rise anew in Christ through the strong participation of the assembly.

Speaking of the assembly, let us not forget that they too have a special role in the Mass and abundant opportunities to manifest the paschal mystery. They are not merely onlookers but offer the sacrifice of the Mass "not only by means of the hands of the Priest but also together with him and so that they may learn to offer their very selves."[50] What does it mean to offer your very self as a member of the assembly? First it means showing up—even on mornings when you'd rather sleep in or when you just don't feel like praying. Once God's grace has brought you to Mass (and you've allowed it to do so), it means joining in the prayers, gestures, postures, processions, and songs with enthusiasm and with an awareness and a desire to be one with the whole assembly. *The GIRM* stresses in several ways the importance of the assembly's unity, urging that any appearance of division be avoided. I knew a young man who wished to show his devotion to the Eucharist at Mass by prostrating himself in the main aisle during the consecration. What effect do you imagine this had on the celebration? It drew all eyes to him and away from the Body and Blood of Christ! As assembly members, we must die to our own dispositions and desires sometimes when they cause us to manifest disunity. In so doing, we rise again as one body in Christ.

The ministry of the lector presents opportunities to die and rise in Christ as well. I heard about a study of people's fears a few years ago. It said the two things that scare people most are death and public speaking. The lector has to overcome one of these fears (not both, we hope!) in order to execute his or her ministry. Lectors must look presentable for their visible role, taking care to dress with modesty and respect for the assembly. They must prepare carefully, rehearsing the readings many times, especially any troublesome pronunciations or complex passages. Lectors do well to ask for and apply feedback from others about their ministry. Most importantly, lectors manifest the paschal mystery by "getting out of the way" and allowing God to use them as a mouthpiece for his holy Word. An attitude of humility is essential. I recently sent an e-mail to a lector at my parish who had read particularly well at Mass, complimenting him on his ministry. I was moved, but not surprised, to read his response: "Thank you, but as you know, my gift comes from God." No wonder he is such a fine lector!

Extraordinary ministers of holy Communion are also manifestations of Christ's paschal mystery in the Mass. They have a humble, inviting presence as they reverently distribute the sacred species to the assembly. They handle the vessels with care and respect, and they assist in the washing of purified vessels after Mass. Though their ministry is less visible than the lector's, they are often recognized as leaders in the faith community by the rest of the assembly and accordingly are sought out to handle concerns or pass on information. They respond to such needs with hospitality and grace, never with resentment or an attitude of "this isn't my job." Sometimes they take on additional duties, such as the distribution of ashes or blessing of throats. By their dignified yet humble leadership, extraordinary ministers of holy Communion show what it means to live a life nourished by the Body and Blood of Christ.

Other special roles—like servers, sacristan, Psalmist, cantor, hospitality ministers, and ushers—all contribute to this great celebration of the paschal mystery we call the Mass. Each has opportunities to participate in the death and resurrection of

Christ in the liturgy. And yet the Mass isn't "about" any one of these roles, even that of the presider. The Mass is "about" Christ and the eternal work of redemption he effected by his death and resurrection: the paschal mystery.

DISCUSSION QUESTIONS

1. *At the Second Vatican Council, what was the debate over use of the vernacular in liturgy like? What were some of the arguments for and against this change?*

2. *The final vote by the bishops of the world ratifying the Constitution on the Sacred Liturgy was 2,147 to 4. Does this lopsidedly affirmative vote surprise you? Why or why not?*

3. *What are some of the most important ideas about liturgy to come from the Constitution on the Sacred Liturgy? Which ideas interested you most and why?*

4. *What does the term* **paschal mystery** *refer to at its most basic level? How could understanding this phrase at a deeper level help us to celebrate the Mass?*

5. *How is Jesus like Moses? How is Jesus the "new Adam?" What do these realities have to do with the term* **paschal mystery***?*

6. *Why did Pope Benedict XVI say that the love Christ teaches by his paschal mystery is "love in its most radical form?" What makes it so radical?*

7. *How is the paschal mystery revealed in the Church's sacramental celebrations?*

8. *How is the paschal mystery revealed in the liturgical year?*

9. *How is the paschal mystery revealed in the various ministries of the Mass?*

CHAPTER 4
On the Threshold:
Introductory Rites of Mass

LIMINAL SPACE

Several years ago I attended a conference for ministry professionals, and a notion from one of the keynote addresses stuck with me. The speaker's overarching message was about conversion: not necessarily conversion to Christ, for the audience members were Christians already. He was talking about conversion to greater holiness and how we as ministers can best assist the Holy Spirit in making people more holy. Specifically, he spoke of fostering the kind of atmosphere that promotes such conversion, calling it "liminal space." The word "liminal" comes from the Latin word *limen* for "threshold." The phrase "liminal space" refers to the sort of space where change can occur: where hearts are open to the kind of conversion to which God is calling them. It is the opposite of what Jesus called "hardness of heart" in the Gospel. It is space where hearts are disposed to hear God's word and to accept and celebrate God's gifts.

I particularly like the way the phrase makes us imagine ourselves standing on a threshold leading from one space to another. Thresholds are important symbols, especially in churches. The physical doors that admit the assembly into the worship space for Mass have both functional and symbolic purposes, as the U.S. Catholic Bishops' directives on church architecture state.[51] Their functional purpose is obvious, but as symbols they remind us of Jesus, who in Matthew's Gospel urges his followers to enter heaven through the "narrow gate" that leads to life, and who in John's Gospel calls himself *the* way to the Father: the *only* way to God. Doors and thresholds, especially in churches, help us remember the liminal space that Jesus not only creates but becomes for his people, the Church.

This notion of "liminal space" and the symbolic nature of doorways is useful in getting at the character and purpose of the Introductory Rites of the Mass. In the 2011 *GIRM*, the Introductory Rites are said to "have the character of a beginning, an introduction, and a preparation. Their purpose is to ensure that the faithful, who come together as one, establish communion and dispose themselves properly to listen to the Word of God and to celebrate the Eucharist worthily."[52] The Introductory Rites are not why we gather—we gather to hear God's Word and to celebrate his sacrament. Thus the Introductory Rites are less significant, and certainly less ancient, than the Liturgies of Word and Eucharist that follow. (Mass is a great complex of rites, and although none are unimportant, each individual rite is not necessarily equal to the others in importance.) The Introductory Rites developed and became a stable part of the Roman Rite by the early Middle Ages, probably in answer to our human need for a point of beginning to such an important event as our Sunday worship. Thus the significance of the rituals we perform at the beginning of each Mass lies in their ability to create that "liminal space" that gathers us as one and disposes us for the more important things we are about to do.

But why do we need to be "properly disposed" to celebrate the Mass? Is the world inside our celebration so very different from the one outside? Yes and no. Yes: Everything from the inside of the church building (one hopes) to the language and content of the ritual is designed to call our hearts and minds to the consideration of holy things—to the worship of God and to participation in his great paschal mystery—in a way very unlike the outside world. Our liturgy ingrains in us an appreciation for—even an ability to recognize in the first place—the presence of God in signs: gestures, songs, vessels, vestments, water, food, and drink. At the same time, recognition and appreciation of God's presence in the signs of our faith creates in us the potential to see *all* the world as filled with the presence of God. So the water that is blessed and used for baptism, in which we bless ourselves as we enter the church, can train us to see the water shooting from a city fire hydrant as an echo of that same sign of God's healing powers of making things new and filling us with life. Especially when that fire hydrant has attracted seventeen formerly bored and hot children, now having the time of their lives, this sort of "small s" sacramental sign can show us something of the delight and refreshment God brings to our sweltering lives. And the children themselves can remind us of the exuberant eagerness with which we are called to accept such gifts from God, who wants us to receive him with the trust and innocence of such as these.

I hope you'll allow me to pursue what may seem like a digression a little further so as to make my point. By calling the Introductory Rites of Mass "liminal space" and comparing them to a threshold, I do not want to suggest that they strip us of all vestiges of the world outside before we enter into the holy act of Mass. Rather, we cross the threshold just as we are, and we bring what we have to the celebration. We are both material and spiritual beings, we humans, with both body and soul, and we bring our whole selves before the Lord in worship. This is nothing to be ashamed of! God-in-Christ has justified and affirmed the material world by his Incarnation and participation in our human life: by his paschal mystery, which is the redemption of the world. As we begin each celebration of his paschal mystery, we enter into a holier place that trains our eyes to recognize God's presence all around us. But we do so knowing that that threshold awaits us once again after Mass. When we reemerge into the "outside" world, it will look different to our eyes, which have been given the power to see God's presence there, too. Far from divesting ourselves of the world around us, learning to hope in—and work for—the world's greater holiness is part of how we become properly disposed to celebrate the Mass.

This is no easy task! Seeing the holiness of the world is not something the dominant secular, capitalist culture promotes. In fact, we are urged to see our world as dangerous, others as untrustworthy, and ourselves as in constant need of physical and financial improvement. One person, disposed by the liturgy to see the world the way God sees it, faces an uphill battle. This brings us to the other important purpose of the Introductory Rites of Mass: Besides disposing our hearts to properly celebrate the Eucharist, the beginning of Mass functions to make us one. No matter what some televangelists and Christian pop songs might claim, God-in-Christ did not come to be each human being's "personal savior"; rather, he came that all may be one, as he is one with the Father (John 17:21). As *one* people he saves us: He makes us into *one* body in himself, for salvation is not simply about being saved—it is about being *sent* as well. In the paschal mystery, we are both saved and sent to do Christ's work, and our Savior knows we cannot do this alone. Therefore, *The GIRM* says the Introductory Rites of Mass "establish Communion" [53] among the faithful who have gathered: a collection of "I"s is invited to become a "we." As the celebration of Mass begins, we as individuals are invited to step across the threshold and become a Church.

THE STRUCTURE OF THE INTRODUCTORY RITES

The Entrance

What better way to begin the Introductory Rites, which undertake to unify and dispose us for the celebration at hand, than in song? The entrance chant (sometimes known as the opening hymn or song) refers to the music that accompanies the entrance procession of the ministers of the Mass. This music can be a hymn, song, chant, or musical setting of the given psalm antiphon from the *Roman Gradual*, which is the book containing the chant texts for the celebration of Mass in given seasons and on particular occasions (votive Masses, saints' feasts, etc.).

The GIRM says the purpose of the entrance chant is "to open the celebration, foster the unity of those who have been gathered, introduce their thoughts to the mystery of the liturgical time or festivity, and accompany the procession of the Priest and ministers."[54] The choice of the music for the entrance chant usually falls to the music minister or ministers and is an important decision. If they do not choose to use a musical setting of the assigned antiphon of the day from the *Roman Gradual*, the chosen song or hymn should have clear and obvious references to the liturgical season or scriptural themes of the day, especially the Gospel. At the same time, the music must be accessible to the assembly so they may sing together with confidence. Using an obscure hymn that sets the Gospel for the day to music may not be a good choice if the assembly is unfamiliar with that piece and cannot sing it readily: better to use a familiar song with themes of gathering and unity instead. Finally, music ministers must remember the more practical purpose of the music at the opening of Mass: to accompany the procession of ministers as they enter the worship space. The song should not end precipitously after a verse or two but be permitted to play out until all the ministers have entered and taken their places for the celebration. Thus a very short song or chant, however seasonally or topically appropriate, is not usually a good choice for the entrance chant.

Speaking of the entrance procession, it also holds deep significance as part of the Introductory Rites. Lawrence Johnson says it developed as the Eucharist began to be celebrated in large buildings as a natural way to use the space for worship. It obviously had a practical function: to get the ministers of the Mass from the sacristy (often located by the main entrance of the church) to the altar, moving them through the gathered assembly.[55] Though the practice fell into disuse for some time, it is restored in the modern liturgy and takes its place at most Masses as part of the Introductory Rites.

If you attend daily Mass, you may see only the priest in procession, and he may make a simple entrance from somewhere near the sanctuary; this is legitimate and appropriate. But on Sundays, and especially on high solemnities, the procession is more distinguished and elaborate, which tells the assembly as Mass begins that something especially significant is about to occur. Though it can take many forms, a more complex entrance procession in the average parish begins with a thurifer— that is, a server or acolyte carrying incense to "sweeten the way" for the ministers to follow. The incense also is to be used by the priest to reverence the altar and cross upon arrival in the sanctuary. Then three more servers follow, walking abreast. The two outside carry lighted candles and the middle server bears the processional cross. After them come any other servers or ministers, then a lector with the Book of the Gospels (if there is no deacon), held high so the assembly may see. Finally come the priest-presider and any assisting deacons, side-by-side (the deacon who proclaims the Gospel would carry the book instead of the lector and go before the presider). Again, an entrance procession may have fewer elements than this (and in some cases more), but for particularly important Sunday celebrations (such as Easter or Pentecost) and other solemnities (such as Christmas or All Saints), this is the standard form of the entrance procession.

The image of people in motion, undertaking a journey or pilgrimage, has always been important to Christians. Jesus himself was a man in motion, traveling back and forth throughout the regions of Jews and Gentiles, spreading the Gospel message. His deliberate journey to Jerusalem and to the cross in the Gospels has long been a subject of study and reflection for theologians. So it was natural for the practice of procession to make its way into the symbol set of the Christian liturgy.

In the later Middle Ages, the pious practice of making pilgrimage became an important part of both the religious imagination and even the economy of Christian Europe. Curiosity, devotion, and vigorous penances drove medieval Catholics to explore the religious sites of the Holy Land and other places of spiritual significance. This created a pilgrim culture with particular etiquette, gear, and rituals of sending pilgrims forth. Eventually establishments along pilgrimage routes sprung up that catered to the holy travelers, providing preparations and cautions for travelers, as medieval roads could be dangerous places.

Most of all, the medieval pilgrim culture held that the journey is as important as the destination. It was "on the way" that a pilgrim attained greater holiness, arriving at his destination more ready to devote himself to God through the experience of his journey. The Second Vatican Council revisited this age-old image of pilgrimage as a way of describing the people of God who make up the Church, and this description of our identity has become an important way in which the modern Church understands itself. In The Dogmatic Constitution on the Church (*Lumen Gentium*), the major document on the Church (like the CSL but addressing the nature of the Church instead of the nature of its liturgy), the council describes with great beauty the way in which the Church is a pilgrim people, making its way home to God:

> The Church, "like a stranger in a foreign land, presses
> forward amid the persecutions of the world and the
> consolations of God," announcing the cross and death
> of the Lord until he comes (1 Corinthians 11:26). But

by the power of the risen Lord she is given strength to overcome, in patience and in love, her sorrows and her difficulties, both those that are from within and those that are from without, so that she may reveal in the world, faithfully, however darkly, the mystery of her Lord until, in the consummation, it shall be manifested in full light.[56]

Far from supposing that the only true holiness lies in heaven, the notion of pilgrimage in Catholic culture is yet another example of our passionate belief in the potential for the material world around us to be a source of God's presence among us and an opportunity to grow in holiness.

This is why every procession within Mass holds rich significance as a sign of our identity as the people of God and of God's presence within and among us, and the entrance procession is no different. Even the different ministers within the procession are symbolic. The thurifer with incense goes before the rest with a symbol of prayer and reverence that hearkens back to Roman imperial culture and the honors that accompanied civic leaders. At the same time it is a sign of sacrifice, and the smell of incense often turns people's senses immediately to the holy. (When I burn it in my house someone usually remarks, "it smells like church in here!") Then comes another great sign of sacrifice: the processional cross, flanked on either side by light. Who comes in this procession? None other than Christ's paschal mystery of death and resurrection, which brings the light by which all people walk in God's ways. Then, after other miscellaneous ministers, comes the Word of the Lord, held high by the one who is to proclaim it. In the liturgy, God's Word comes among us, comes through us, and remains with us. (The Gospel Book, you will note, is never carried back out of church in the concluding procession!) Finally come the priest-presider and any concelebrants (other priests who are not presiding) and assisting deacons. The priest comes last because he is in the person of Christ among the assembly, and at the same time he represents the assembly *to* the Father, in the name of Christ, in the prayers of the liturgy. He is a true sign of the sacrament—Eucharist—that is to be celebrated that day. (For the Rite of Marriage, the rubrics call for the bride and groom to come last in the procession, because they represent the sign of the sacrament—matrimony—which is to be celebrated *that* day.)

The entrance procession moves slowly, gracefully, and deliberately through the worship space, with purpose but without haste. Each pilgrim in the procession should know in advance exactly where he or she is headed, and those who are not carrying anything make a reverential bow to the altar as they move to their ultimate position for Mass. This bow is called a *profound* bow: a bow from the waist, as opposed to one from the neck (that would be a *simple* bow). Those carrying objects deposit them where they belong (candles into candle holders, cross into its stand, etc.) as the ordained ministers gather behind the altar to venerate it with a kiss. This is an ancient symbol of reverence used for temples and images of gods in pagan culture. In Christian usage it acknowledges that the altar, usually made of stone, is the great physical symbol of Christ, whom Scripture calls the "cornerstone," in the worship space. Then when incense is used, the priest takes the incense from the thurifer and walks around the altar, reverencing it with holy smoke. He incenses the cross as well, then the incense is removed from the sanctuary and the presider moves to his chair. At this point, the entrance chant or hymn should be nearly complete.

The Sign of the Cross, Greeting, and Introduction

Next come two very important pieces of the Introductory Rites: the Sign of the Cross and greeting. When the entrance song is at an end, the priest-presider, together with the whole gathered assembly, makes the Sign of the Cross. By so doing we express in whose name we are gathered and for what purpose: in the Blessed Trinity of Father, Son, and Holy Spirit in order for God to make present in us the death and resurrection of his Christ. We mark ourselves with the Sign of the Cross because we know ourselves, each other, our lives, and our community to be permanently marked, by virtue of our baptism, by this mystery we share. There is no need for "Good morning!" or another everyday greeting because what we gather to do is decidedly not everyday, and social niceties in this profound moment threaten to cheapen the experience. And so the deliberateness and grace with which we sign ourselves with the cross in the name of the Holy Trinity bespeak the deliberateness and grace with which the life of God animates us as individuals and as a community. Avoid the appearance, when you are making the Sign of the Cross, of swatting away flies!

The next rite to occur is very ancient within our liturgical tradition and significant not just to the Introductory Rites but to the whole celebration of Mass: the greeting. The priest says to the assembly, "The Lord be with you," and the people respond, "And with your spirit." *The GIRM* says, "by this greeting and the people's response, the mystery of the Church gathered together is made manifest."[57] Wow! Really? This ancient formula has a rock-solid basis in both Hebrew and Christian Scriptures, both as a greeting and also as way of acknowledging God's presence in the persons greeted. Its words are lifted directly from Scripture (the people's response comes from Paul's letters) and signifies both our acknowledgment and intention that God is present here and now in the assembly and in the presider, who has received the Spirit of God in ordination in a special way, in order to serve the people of God in the liturgy. The words of greeting used by the presider can vary; there are a few textual options in the *Missal* and a few additional options when the bishop presides. Note that this greeting is repeated at five different points within the celebration of Mass—this also denotes its importance to our identity as the body of Christ, gathered to manifest the paschal mystery.

Following this greeting, a few words of introduction to the Mass of the day, the occasion, or the particular community gathered are permissible. Lawrence Johnson says this should not be a homily preview or a repetition of the greeting.[58] Presiders should avoid the colloquial, "Good morning, everybody!" at this point too, as if the liturgical greeting acknowledging God's presence among us did not suffice. Rather, as befits its inclusion in the Introductory Rites as a whole, these brief words of introduction should help the assembly turn their hearts and minds more fully to the mysteries of which we will hear in Scripture and celebrate in the Eucharist.

The Penitential Act

There are a few different ways the assembly can make a penitential act for their sinfulness, as is called for next in the Introductory Rites. They can say the *Confiteor*, led by the presider ("I confess to Almighty God…"), or join in a dialogue with the presider based on scriptural verses from Baruch and Psalm 85 ("Have mercy on us, O Lord…"). This is followed by the *Kyrie, eleison* ("Lord, have mercy") or a musical chant of the *Kyrie* with "tropes" (phrases that introduce and amplify the text). In whatever form, the penitential act is concluded by the presider's absolution, which, as *The GIRM* puts it, "lacks the efficacy of the Sacrament of Penance."[59] (This is why we do not sign ourselves at this point in Mass, even if we do when receiving absolution in the sacrament of penance.)

But what may be more on the mind of someone learning about the different rites of Mass and how they fit together is this: Why talk about sin right out of the liturgical gate? In fact, why talk of sin at all in the context of Mass? Isn't that part of a *different* sacrament, reconciliation? At Mass, haven't we gathered to *celebrate* God's gift to us in the Eucharist? Doesn't all this talk of our sinfulness put a damper on our festivity?

It is true, says Lawrence Johnson, that for centuries the Mass did not include a penitential rite. But in Scripture and early Christian writings, there is a clear indication of the need to confess our sins and reconcile with one another before celebrating the Eucharist, and this is why a simple penitential rite appears in the post-Vatican II liturgy.[60] A look at some of its elements helps explain its significance within the Introductory Rites of Mass. First the assembly is invited by the presider to recall its sinfulness, and silence to enable this reflection follows. Then the presider makes a proclamation that we are all sinners before God. This is a profound admission that none of us is above sinfulness, that each of us has something for which we are ashamed. In one sense it is refreshingly honest; instead of constantly attempting to make ourselves into more than we are (and more than the next person) as our society encourages, we stand before God with both our virtues and our vices. In this sense we make an honest offering, and we are all equals in our admission of guilt. In addition, the scriptural dialogue option ("Have mercy on us, O Lord/For we have sinned against you"), we express that we have *together* sinned against God. Sinfulness is not simply individual people making bad choices but systems of injustice, greed, and fearful hatred. They are perhaps not designed to do harm, but at best such human systems ignore the harm done. This also is part of what we bring before God.

What a downer! When we think about the many dimensions of our sinfulness, we may want to run away from God's presence, fearing we are unworthy. But at its core, the Act of Penitence in Mass is more about God's mercy than about our sinfulness. It is a wondrous expression of confidence that God's mercy is far wider than our worst faults and is able and ready to swallow both us and our sins up in the vastness of his love and forgiveness. The Act of Penitence, therefore, fits well with the purpose of the Introductory Rites: to ready ourselves for the celebration of the paschal mystery by unburdening ourselves of the weight of our sins, which God makes light.

Sunday Renewal of Baptism

Sometimes, however, it does seem more appropriate to keep the focus of the Introductory Rites firmly on the joy of the resurrection, and this is why, "from time to time on Sundays, especially in Easter Time, instead of the customary Penitential Act, the blessing and sprinkling of water may take place as a reminder of Baptism."[61] In this option, the presider processes through the assembly, sprinkling it with holy water, usually accompanied by a song about baptism. This substitution of a rite of sprinkling for the penitential rite is especially appropriate during the Easter season, when newly baptized members celebrate in full communion with the whole assembly, who themselves have just made the Easter renewal of baptism. However, the sprinkling rite can be used on any Sunday (but not every Sunday). There are many such choices among the rites of Mass, and this one highlights the paschal character of our worship: our liberation from sin and death by the mercy and strength of God.

The Glory to God

It is only appropriate, after we have asked for and acknowledged God's great mercy in the Act of Penitence, or renewed our baptism with a sprinkling rite, to sing together a hymn of Glory to God. This very ancient song of praise began as an Easter hymn but eventually made its way into more frequent use. Now it is sung on all Sundays, solemnities, and feasts outside the seasons of Lent and Advent, because those seasons call us to a sort of ritual fasting in order to heighten the solemnity of the seasons that follow (Easter and Christmas). The text of the Glory to God is Trinitarian in nature, and although the priest, choir, or a cantor intones the Glory to God (that is, introduces it by singing the first line), the entire assembly is encouraged to sing along. Its purpose is to sanctify our good God, but the Glory to God also helps to properly dispose us to celebrate the Eucharist by acclaiming God as Three Persons in One: a relationship of holiness in whose image of communion we are formed. This song draws us closer to God whom we praise and into greater union with one another in sharing the life of Father, Son, and Holy Spirit.

The Glory to God should never be skipped in the interests of making Mass shorter or because of a lack of preparation on the part of musicians. In fact, if it is not sung it is to be recited by all. However, due to the nature of the Glory to God itself as a hymn of praise, music-less recitation is not a great option. Its singing should never be a burden or a drag on the Introductory Rites of Mass; if it seems so, it may be time for the community to learn a new musical setting or for catechesis on the hymn and its meaning. The Glory to God should help us remember that Sunday is special: the day of the Lord, whom we praise with all the angels.

The Collect

The what? Oh, you mean the "Let us pray" prayer! Yes, that's it. The final piece of the Introductory Rites of Mass is the Collect, or opening prayer. Each Collect was composed specifically for the celebration at hand, and many Collects have long histories, dating back hundreds and hundreds of years. They are theologically rich and rhetorically fine (if sometimes grammatically complicated), and most ask God to prepare us, in some specific way, to celebrate the mysteries at hand. The GIRM says it well; the Collect is the prayer "through which the character of the celebration finds expression."[62] Why are they called "Collect" prayers? Because they "collect" the many prayers of the gathered assembly into one prayer, proclaimed by the presider. This is why the presider pauses after he says, "Let us pray." This pause is not so the server may bring over the book (though that often happens, too)! It is so that we may remember we are standing in God's presence and bring to mind the prayers in our hearts before the Collect is pronounced, offering them all.

The Collect, like the Glory to God, is Trinitarian in nature. It always ends with a doxology, or a short verse praising God the Father through the Son, and in the Holy Spirit. At the end of the prayer, the assembly "make the prayer their own"[63] by means of their "Amen." We will talk about the rich significance of this acclamation "Amen" later in the book when we discuss the "Great Amen" that follows the Eucharistic Prayer. It suffices for now to say that "Amen" is a very ancient way of pledging one's promise or affirmation on a thing. In the context of our liturgical tradition, "Amen" seals the deal.

Giving our "Amen" to the Collect provides closure not just to the prayer but to the Introductory Rites themselves, which have now ended. We have passed through that "liminal space" of transition and preparation, and our hearts and minds are now readied for the more significant rites to follow in the Liturgy of the Word.

DISCUSSION QUESTIONS

1. What is "liminal space," and what does it have to do with the Introductory Rites of Mass?

2. What is the purpose of the entrance chant or song?

3. What does the notion of pilgrimage in Catholic culture bring to our understanding of the opening procession of Mass? What does the opening procession symbolize?

4. Why is it not necessary for the presider to greet the assembly with a "good morning" during the Introductory Rites?

5. Why is the Penitential Act in Mass more about God's mercy than our own sinfulness?

6. At the Collect prayer, why does the presider pause after he says, "Let us pray?" Does knowing what this pause is for change your perspective on it? How?

CHAPTER 5
The Table Is Spread:
The Liturgy of the Word

The *GIRM* says "in the readings...God speaks to his people, opening up to them the mystery of redemption and salvation, and offering spiritual nourishment; and Christ himself is present through his word in the midst of the faithful." [64] Proclamations from Scripture, their interpretation, and our response are the focus of the next major part of the Mass: the Liturgy of the Word.

This series of proclamations, acclamations, and prayers is not simply a prelude to holy Communion. The Liturgy of the Word and the Liturgy of the Eucharist are integrally related and serve to amplify the power and riches each has to offer those gathered for the celebration. The Liturgy of the Word gives us an effective model of what it means to live the life of God, and the Liturgy of the Eucharist gives us the effective power to do so. [65] The *Introduction to the Lectionary* characterizes their relationship another way: In the Word, the Church grows in wisdom, and in the Eucharist, in holiness. [66] In both Word and sacrament, God nourishes us for our journey home to him. This is why, despite that eating and drinking in a physical sense come later in Mass, *The GIRM* says in the Liturgy of the Word, "the table of God's Word is spread before the faithful." [67]

THE SACRAMENTAL POWER OF WORDS

Perhaps this image of the Word of God as nourishment—as a table spread for all—comes from the Book of Proverbs. In that book's personification of Wisdom, she (for the biblical author speaks of Wisdom as feminine) sets up house, prepares a meal, and sets a table, to which she invites the simple and foolish to join her and "advance in the way of understanding" (Proverbs 9:6b). This connection between God's wisdom and the sustenance we humans need on a daily basis would have imbued the imaginations of those who heard Jesus say, "I am the bread of life; whoever comes to me will never hunger" (John 6:35). Jesus often drove home this point about the wisdom he offers as true food and drink in his many food-related miracles, as well as in his ultimate gift to us: the gift of himself in the Eucharist. But we might have guessed we would receive nourishment in many senses from a Savior who spent the first night of his human existence lying in a manger. (A manger is a food trough for animals!)

So wait: Is it the Scriptures on which we focus in the Liturgy of the Word or Jesus? Doesn't his part come later in Mass, in the Eucharist? As I said, the Liturgies of Word and Eucharist are so interconnected that the answer to this question must be: both. Rather, in the Liturgy of the Word we listen and respond to the proclaimed Scriptures that tell us, in longer form, what is completely and perfectly summed up in Christ. Jesus Christ is the Word of God; he is everything God has to say to us humans. This Word—Jesus—was present, as the Gospel of John says, "in the beginning with God. All things came to be through him, and without him nothing came to be" (John 1:2–3). Before the institution of the Eucharist, before baptism, before Christian marriage or any of the sacraments came the Word: Jesus, the true sacrament of God. The Father speaks to us in Christ, and in this Word, eternal life is effectively promised and given.

Because of this powerful reality of Jesus as God's ultimate Word to humanity, words in general carry significant meaning in the Catholic tradition. This may seem like nothing out of the ordinary; our culture at large seems to value words. We say things like "she gave me her word" to indicate an important pledge, and we value a person who is a "man of his word" because he does what he says he is going to do. This is a fine value, but it's not what I'm talking about when I say words carry significant meaning to Catholics. I mean, more than just carrying weight, in the Catholic sacramental worldview, words can be powerful and effective signs of God in the world. Just as Christ mediates the Father's will to us through his teachings and actions, and just as the sacraments are signs of the grace given to us by God throughout our lives, human language mediates the meaning in our minds and the promises in our hearts, giving them substance and shape.

The foundation for this belief in the sacramental power of words is solidly laid in Scripture. As we saw above from John's Gospel, the Word of God was present at the creation of all things: a creative force, quelling the chaos of uncreation. In the prophetic writings, like Isaiah chapter 61, the prophets were seen to deliver a word to the oppressed which, more than merely announcing their liberation from oppression, seems to enact that liberation as well. In his Letter to the Hebrews, St. Paul calls the Word of God "living and effective, sharper than any two-edged sword, penetrating even between soul and spirit, joints and marrow, and able to discern reflections and thoughts of the heart" (4:12). And recall the first gifts of the Holy Spirit when it descends, like tongues of fire, upon the apostles at Pentecost in the Acts of the Apostles: "They were all filled with the holy Spirit and began to speak in different tongues, as the Spirit enabled them to proclaim" (2:4). Why was the Holy Spirit's first gift to the Church the ability to speak various languages? So that it could proclaim the Good News to diverse groups of people, of course. Words are vehicles for the Gospel in the world.

Words in our tradition are holy, living, and effective. Think of the word "Amen." It has never been translated into English from the Hebrew because there is no term in English to do it justice. "So be it" doesn't cover what we mean when we say "Amen," nor does "I do believe," because "Amen" is both a statement of agreement and affirmation, but also a pledge, a promise, a life-orienting vow to live differently in light of that to which you give your "Amen." It is a word that signifies an intensity of integrity belonging to God alone. St. Augustine told his fourth-century parishioners that when they say "Amen" to the body of Christ in the Eucharist, they are promising to *be* the body of Christ that they are receiving. So *be* the body of Christ, he told them, so that your "Amen" will be true.[68] The same could be said of the words Catholics say in the sacrament of marriage: "I do." These words hold power, are binding, and effective in creating a lifelong union between two people. At the same time they are a promise of commitment that must be backed by the hard work and sacrifice that every marriage requires.

But lest it seem that we humans who utter these powerful words are the ones making them "stick" as it were, let us remember that, like Christ and the sacraments to which words are analogs, the words themselves hold no power without God. Even though we say "Amen" and "I do" in Eucharist and marriage, we do not make ourselves the body of Christ, and we cannot keep our marriages together on our own. Without God, our words have no meaning. God is the power behind all words in the Catholic tradition. But in this world, words stand in as signs for God's will and God's power in our lives. It is this context in which we celebrate the Liturgy of the Word, understanding that God's word is a living, potent, effective force in history and in our individual and collective lives.

This idea of the sacramental power of words in the Catholic tradition is supported and sustained by the formal proclamation of God's Word in the context of the liturgy. Reading the Scriptures, whether as individuals or in the context of a Bible study, is always a good idea. But in Mass, readings from Scripture are not merely *read*, they are *proclaimed*. What's the difference?

First, proclamation suggests *public* reading, as opposed to private or individual reading, which is less of a shared experience. Compare the experience of all your friends reading the same book individually and all your friends sitting in a room together while that same book is read to you aloud. You might all gasp in the same exciting place, share laughter at the funny bits, or exchange knowing glances when trouble arises. In the second scenario, you and your friends share the experience of the story in the moment instead of after the fact. In a similar way, the faithful share an experience of the story of our faith when the Scriptures are proclaimed in Mass. In fact, though the practice of "reading along" with the Scripture proclamations out of a missalette during Mass is widespread, many experts frown on it, because it may individualize the experience of the proclamation for the listener. Proclamation is a communal experience that requires communal listening.

Secondly, a distinction lies in the *power* of proclamation versus reading. Reading is purely functional, like the safety spiel the flight attendants read to the passengers over the intercom before the plane takes off. But proclamation has power, it has spiritual force. Something new takes place when the Word is proclaimed in our midst at Mass. The *Introduction to the Lectionary for Mass* says the Word of God, as it is proclaimed and celebrated in the liturgy, and as the faithful respond to it through the Holy Spirit, becomes a "new event and enriches the word itself with new meaning and power." [69] This new event is a sacramental moment: a sign of God, speaking not just to people long ago, but to us now.

SILENCE

Before we move on to the individual rites within the Liturgy of the Word, something must be said about silence. Brief periods of silence throughout the Liturgy of the Word are recommended by *The GIRM* in order to foster meditation and reflection on the Word of God. More specifically, *The GIRM* says through silence in the liturgy, "under the action of the Holy Spirit, the Word of God may be grasped by the heart and a response through prayer may be prepared."[70] The United States Conference of Catholic Bishops' 2007 instruction on music in liturgy, *Sing to the Lord*, says silence is the vehicle through which the assembly may open their hearts to the mysteries celebrated in the Mass, and therefore its importance cannot be overestimated.

In this sense, silence can be compared to the rest an athlete needs as part of his or her training process. Most serious athletes realize that nonstop training is the best way to achieve not their goals but a debilitating injury. The right amount of rest built in to a rigorous training schedule allows the muscles of the body to benefit from the work they have done and rejuvenate for the work ahead. It is this way with the mind and heart of the worshiping assembly. We cannot go, go, go indefinitely; the mind cannot continue to function if it does not stop to sort, analyze, and reflect upon the information it has received. The heart—what we Westerners think of as the seat of our emotions—is not made just for feeling but also for contemplation on the feelings it experiences. Like an athlete must be responsible for obtaining the rest his body needs, it is up to a believer to take the requisite time out of her busy life to reflect on her relationship with God and to listen to where God might be leading her.

In the liturgy, such time for reflection is built in: before the readings begin, after the first and second readings, and after the homily.[71] As an added bonus, this back-and-forth pattern of words and silence helps give the Liturgy of the Word its distinctive rhythm.[72] However, over time a community can forget to value these periods of silence, and they can become shortened or eliminated altogether. It is up to liturgists, presiders, and lectors to preserve these times of silence so that the Word of God proclaimed in the Scriptures and interpreted in the homily may have the proper space and time to resonate in the heart of the body of Christ.

THE STRUCTURE OF THE LITURGY OF THE WORD

Readings, Acclamations, Ambo

The Liturgy of the Word is laid out for us in the *Lectionary*, or the book of scriptural readings to be proclaimed in Mass. The *Lectionary* contains the segments of the readings to be proclaimed in the proper order for each Sunday and weekday Mass. After the Second Vatican Council, the *Lectionary* was arranged so that a great deal more of the riches of the Bible would be laid out for the faithful than previously. Before the council the same cycle of readings repeated each year; now there is a three-year cycle of readings for Sunday Mass and a two-year cycle for weekdays (we name them A, B, C, and I, II respectively). The first reading and responsorial psalm were chosen to correspond to the Gospel of the day. In the case of the New Testament writings (the second reading) and the Gospel, the readings flow chronologically. (For instance, in year "A" we work our way chronologically through Matthew's Gospel; in year "B" we move on to Mark, etc., and John's Gospel is used primarily in the Easter season for all three years.) However, this neat and tidy arrangement of the readings is interrupted in the seasons. In Advent, Christmas, Lent, and Easter, all the readings correspond to one another and draw out the mysteries of the season within its larger context, the paschal mystery.

In addition to the readings, the *Lectionary* also contains the texts and acclamations that relate to them. These serve to introduce the reading ("A reading from the Book of..."), to conclude it by professing to the assembly that God's holy word has indeed been proclaimed ("the word of the Lord"), and to allow the assembly to "give honor to the Word of God that they have received in faith and with gratitude"[73] ("Thanks be to God"). These simple acclamations do not need elaboration or alteration by the lector; this only distracts the assembly needlessly and draws attention to the lector as an individual. They are simple for a reason: to function well while leaving room for a more elaborate set of acclamations before the Gospel. These include the sung *Alleluia* with a Scripture verse, then the greeting and response before the Gospel proclamation, wherein the assembly acknowledges, as they did at the beginning of Mass, the Lord's presence with and among them.

One more note before we walk through the Liturgy of the Word, on the ambo. The word comes from Greek and refers to a mountain or elevation, such as Jesus might have stood on to deliver his Sermon on the Mount. The ambo is the lectern or reading-stand reserved for the proclamation of Scripture in Mass, including the responsorial psalm, as well as the homily. It is one of the principle ritual furnishings in the worship space and should have a dignity and formality appropriate to its purpose. The ambo is not a good place from which to read announcements or other parish business, because this takes away something of its unique dignity as the "table of the Word" on which the scriptural feast is spread. The ambo is not, however, as important as the altar, which serves as a symbol of Christ, the cornerstone. This is why ministers reverence the altar with a profound bow, but not the ambo. The ambo is the focal point throughout the Liturgy of the Word.

The First Reading

After a brief period of preparatory silence, a lector proclaims the first reading from Scripture. Outside of the Easter season, this reading is taken from the Hebrew Scriptures, or the Old Testament. (In Easter we hear stories of the resurrected Christ, usually from the Acts of the Apostles.) The Old Testament reading, in some way, relates to the Gospel proclamation for the day. Together, these two passages reveal a particular aspect of the continuity and completeness Jesus brings to the faith of our ancestors, the

Jewish people. The first reading is a great gift of the Second Vatican Council. Before the council one heard only about one percent of the Old Testament in the course of regular Mass attendance. Now its riches are spread for us each Sunday at the table of God's Word.

Lectors should keep this gift in mind as they prepare both the first and second readings, keeping a slow and deliberate pace, to allow the assembly to savor the words they proclaim, as if they were savoring a delicious meal. In the same way, the acclamation that concludes the reading, "the Word of the Lord," should not be permitted to become routine or mechanical, such that it is garbled or pronounced without reverence (for example, "thewordatheLord"). Instead it should be said, or even chanted on a simple tone, as a profession of faith, as if to say, "in what I just proclaimed before you, God spoke!" This might sound something like: "the Word [pause] of the Lord." To such a deliberate and reverent invitation can the assembly truly cry in gratitude: "Thanks be to God!"

The Responsorial Psalm

The responsorial psalm, as *The GIRM* puts it, "is an integral part of the Liturgy of the Word and...has great liturgical and pastoral importance, since it fosters meditation on the Word of God."[74] This is because it both is the Word of God (almost always taken from the Old Testament psalms) and it points to the Word of God as proclaimed in the other Scripture readings at Mass. In addition, it is set to music that enhances the text and draws out the emotion the psalm conveys. These combined factors make the psalm one of the most dramatic and effective pieces of the Liturgy of the Word. There is a strong preference for it to be sung, since the psalms of the Bible are inherently musical, and for it to be participatory, inviting the assembly to join in the antiphon of the psalm (pop music fans might think of this as the "refrain" that repeats between the verses). However, even if there is no one to lead the singing of the psalm, it is still included in the Liturgy of the Word but recited by the lector and assembly instead. The back-and-forth or dialogic nature of the psalm echoes and enhances the dialogic rhythm of the Liturgy of the Word as a whole.

How does the responsorial psalm point to the other Scripture readings of the Mass? It is chosen, especially in its antiphon, with the first reading in mind. Therefore it relates to the Gospel as well. The particular way in which it relates to these other two readings varies from Sunday to Sunday, but Massgoers who are really paying attention may notice that it seems to articulate an emotional response to the first reading. Some scholars have referred to the responsorial psalm as creating a "bridge" of meaning from the first reading to the Gospel.

One note on the musical setting for the responsorial psalm. Because the psalm is essentially one of the readings from Scripture, the choice of musical setting should be made with fidelity to the received translation of the psalm from the *Lectionary*, especially its antiphon (or "refrain"). Some composers take liberties with scriptural texts when setting them to music, and this can result in a beautiful piece of music, but sometimes the meaning or emphasis of the scriptural text is altered in the process. Such a piece would not be an appropriate setting of the responsorial psalm to use during the Liturgy of the Word. (However, such a song may be a good choice for the hymn at the preparation of gifts later in the Mass.) We do not paraphrase the other readings during Mass, so why would we do so for the responsorial psalm?

The need for a musical setting that accommodates the received translation of the psalm often leads to the use of "plainchant," or a simple, nonmetered chant tone, for the verses of the psalm. Plainchant, an ancient and beautiful way of praying sung texts in the Christian tradition, works well to accommodate the text faithfully while adorning it with music so as to bring out its emotive meaning. At the same time, plainchant settings, unlike some modern musical settings of the psalms, are rarely so grand as to outshine the other unsung readings, making the psalm seem like the high point in the Liturgy of the Word (nope, that would be the Gospel). This is why, after centuries of use in liturgy, plainchant has never gone out of style.

The Second Reading

At all Sunday Masses, a reading from the New Testament writings comes after the psalm and before the Gospel Acclamation in the Liturgy of the Word. Neither *The GIRM* nor the *Introduction to the Lectionary for Mass* have much to say specifically about the second reading, but we know it is a "semi-continuous" reading from the many New Testament letters and writings (other than the Gospels, of course). This means we read through a particular letter or book in a continuous way from week to week, skipping some passages (hence, "*semi*-continuous").

The majority of these passages are taken from St. Paul's writings, which provide both blessing and challenge. Unlike the Gospels, they do not usually tell a story but rather are St. Paul's letters of encouragement and instruction to the Christian communities he founded. Many times they sound like they could be written to our community, because Christians today face many of the same challenges as our forebears. Sometimes these letters explain some facet of theology surrounding the person of Jesus or his paschal mystery. This makes them, at times, trying to the attention span, with long, complex, and theologically dense sentences. Lectors must take this into account, preparing the reading carefully so as to bring the emphases that make its meaning accessible to listeners.

The Gospel Acclamation, Gospel, and Homily

In the Mass, there are many different forms of liturgical music, and some are more important than others. The Gospel Acclamation (often known as the *Alleluia*, from a Hebrew word for "praise ye God") ranks among the most important pieces of our liturgical singing because, unlike other pieces that merely accompany actions or rites, it is a rite in itself. Because the Gospel Acclamation is a rite, all members of the assembly sing it together, after it is intoned or introduced by the cantor or choir. It is not meant to be a solo piece but rather a "sing-along," for, as the *Introduction to the Lectionary* says, "it serves as the assembled faithful's greeting of welcome to the Lord who is about to speak to them."[75] However, the Gospel Acclamation has an assigned verse, usually sung by the choir or cantor alone, that calls to mind the themes of the season or the Gospel that day. This is followed by a repetition of the *Alleluia* acclamation.

The importance given to the Gospel Acclamation by our liturgical rubrics tells us much more about the proclamation of the Gospel, really. As we have already seen, all the Scriptures proclaimed in the Liturgy of the Word are, in reality, God speaking to his Church in the midst of the gathered assembly. And although all the readings are important because of this reality, the proclamation of the Gospel embodies this sacramental encounter between God and us most completely. This Gospel Word is Christ, the Wisdom of God incarnate, come among us to instruct and save. Our worship communicates this reality and our response to it in the many symbols, gestures, and actions that surround the proclamation of the Gospel: The sung acclamation that precedes it; the posture of standing that all adopt; the procession with the Gospel Book (itself a special, adorned volume) accompanied by lights and sometimes incense; the kiss of the book by the deacon or presider; the invitation dialogue affirming the Lord's presence in and with us; and the gesture of signing our forehead, mouth, and breast to show our intention that this Word be always on our minds, on our lips, and in our hearts. To show even greater reverence for this moment of encounter between Christ and his Church, the dialogues before and after the Gospel, and even the Gospel itself, may be sung on a simple chant tone.

Next comes the homily, wherein the presider (or deacon or concelebrating priest) breaks open the mysteries proclaimed in the Gospel and the other Scriptures, connecting the Word with our celebration of Christ's eucharistic sacrifice so that the assembly may celebrate the paschal mystery wholeheartedly.[76] This is a tall order! A great homily does all this while grabbing and keeping the assembly's attention (keeping in mind it is made up of all manner of people, from the highly educated to the uneducated, from the very old to the very young, etc.), and without being too long or too short. These requirements necessarily make it, as the *Introduction to the Lectionary* says, "the fruit of meditation, carefully prepared."[77] The homily is never a good time for community announcements or other words that do not foster the celebration at hand; a time for such words is duly set aside after Communion. Because the homily interprets and augments the rich fare of the proclaimed Scriptures in the Liturgy of the Word, it is appropriate for a period of silence to follow it. This provides the assembly the opportunity to "take the word of God to heart and to prepare a response to it in prayer."[78]

The Profession of Faith

In its final two rites, the Liturgy of the Word makes a shift. To this point, we have proclaimed and reflected on sacred Scripture; now in our worship we respond to what we've heard in God's holy Word. Our response as such is twofold: profession and petition.

The "profession" part of our response comes in the Creed. After the homily and that important (if brief) moment of silence, the assembly together, led by the presider (or, if sung, by choir or cantor), professes either the Nicene or the Apostles' Creed. The Creed is a part of Mass on Sundays and solemnities, and, according to *The GIRM*, at Masses of a more solemn character.[79]

Each of these two Creeds is an ancient symbol of the Christian faith: a summary of the story that holds us as believers. Though each Creed reads a bit like a list, neither should be added to or subtracted from, for each has a narrative character that would be altered by doing so. The Creeds first arose both to help new Christians learn the tenets of the faith and as a way of regularizing Christian belief in the face of heresies or irreconcilably different ways of believing. The Creeds sum up the mystery of faith itself. Because of their narrative quality, Creeds are inextricably connected to the Scriptures we celebrate in the Liturgy of the Word, and our profession of the Creed responds to our reflection on the Word by affirming our belief, not just in the passages we've heard that particular day but in the overarching story of our salvation that is poured forth in the pages of the Bible. Theologian Nicholas Lash articulates this connection between the Creeds and the Scriptures succinctly: What the Scriptures say at length, he says, Creeds say in brief.[80]

The Universal Prayer or Prayer of the Faithful

Our second response to the Word we've celebrated in the Liturgy of the Word is that of petition. In the Universal Prayer we, as one priestly people and by virtue of our baptism,[81] make our prayers known, in general and specific ways, to God. This ancient rite is yet another great gift of the Second Vatican Council, which restored them to their proper place in the Mass after centuries of disuse.

These petitions, which conclude the Liturgy of the Word, have been known throughout their long history by a few different names. They are called the Prayer of the Faithful because in the ancient Church they followed the dismissal of the catechumens: those in the process of becoming full members (or part of "the faithful") through baptism. This ancient practice of dismissing the catechumens prior to these prayers of petition, which usually included intentions for the catechumens themselves, tells us something of the prayers' importance to the earliest Christians. (Their form echoes a mandate from St. Paul in his First Letter to Timothy (2:1–4), and early Church apologist St. Justin the Martyr mentions these prayers as well; such early and authoritative references confirm these are indeed important prayers.) Also, the Prayer of the Faithful is a name that points to the specific nature of the petitions. They offer a chance for the local faithful to articulate their particular needs. To facilitate this, no specific wording of the petitions and responses is prescribed by the ritual books, so usually parishes compose their own Prayer of the Faithful.

These petitions are also commonly called the General Intercessions or the Universal Prayer. Both names point to the broad focus of the prayers themselves. This broad focus is a significant attribute of the Prayer of the Faithful that should not be forgotten, because it affects the way the prayers function ritually: That is, they connect the local, gathered community through prayer with the larger, universal Catholic Church. Of course each parish or worshiping community is connected in many ways through its worship to the Church universal, but these petitions offer us a chance to boldly articulate this connection and to concern ourselves and our prayers with not only our own, specific needs, but also the needs of the larger world.

I once worked at a parish that had a tradition of inviting individual members of the assembly to improvise personal petitions over a microphone, to each of which the assembly would respond "Lord, hear our prayer." This practice allowed the community to get to know individual people's struggles and offer help to those who were suffering. However, the General Intercessions took about twenty-five minutes each Sunday (a good deal longer than the Eucharistic Prayer, which as a rite holds far more significance) and kept the parish focused squarely on the needs of its *own* people, instead of challenging it to look beyond its walls to the needs of the larger Church and world. In that parish, the *General* Intercessions were too specific; the *Universal* Prayer was too focused on the local Church. The General Intercessions must balance the twofold reality that each parish or worshiping community is a *particular* incarnation of the *universal* Church.

To assist parishes in striking this balance between the particular and the universal in the Prayer of the Faithful, the ritual books offer content guidelines. According to *The GIRM*, in the Prayer of the Faithful, parishes should pray "for holy Church, for those who govern with authority over us, for those weighed down by various needs, for all humanity, and for the salvation of the whole world."[82] These very general guidelines offer guidance, but also plenty of freedom so that communities may achieve both a local and universal focus to their Prayer of the Faithful. Because the petitions are concerned with the needs of the poor, sick, and oppressed, their presentation is entrusted to the local deacon, whose ministry in the earliest Church was particularly concerned with these least among the community.[83] In the absence of a deacon, a lector reads them.

In the Letter of James, it says, "Be doers of the word and not hearers only" (1:22). In the Liturgy of the Word, we hear and celebrate the Word of God and respond to it in profession and prayer. But it is the Holy Spirit's presence in our liturgical celebrations that "makes that response effective, so that what is heard in the celebration of the Liturgy may be carried out in a way of life."[84] In the seamless act of worship that is the Mass, the *Liturgy of Word* and the Liturgy of the Eucharist are one banquet of good news and thanksgiving. The *Introduction to the Lectionary* says the Church honors the Word and sacrament with the same reverence, if not the same worship. In the next chapter, we will explore how our worship differs in the Liturgy of the Eucharist as we celebrate, receive, and become Christ's perfect embodiment of God's Word.

DISCUSSION QUESTIONS

1. *What does it mean to say that words have "sacramental power" in the Catholic tradition? What gives words this power?*

2. *What is the difference between "reading" and "proclamation?"*

3. *Why is silence an important part of the Mass?*

4. *How do the readings at Mass (first reading, responsorial psalm, second reading, Gospel) relate to one another?*

5. *What is the purpose of the homily? What do you think would be the most challenging part about preparing a homily for presiders or deacons?*

6. *What are some of the various names for the petitions that follow the creed, and what do those names tell us about the petitions themselves?*

CHAPTER 6

The Mystery Meaning You:
The Liturgy of the Eucharist

> From the liturgy, therefore, and especially from the
> Eucharist, as from a font, grace is poured forth upon
> us; and the sanctification of men in Christ and the
> glorification of God, to which all other activities of the
> Church are directed as toward their end, is achieved in
> the most efficacious possible way.
>
> — VATICAN II, CONSTITUTION ON THE SACRED LITURGY
> (*SACROSANCTUM CONCILIUM*), ¶10

From the very dawn of the Church, Christians have celebrated the Eucharist as Christ taught them at the Last Supper, in memory of him. Thus when we consider the Liturgy of the Eucharist, we are considering something most ancient, most holy, and something uniquely Christian. Indeed, we are considering that which lies at the very heart of the Christian faith.

In the earliest celebrations, the Eucharist was celebrated in the context of a meal. This, after all, was the way Jesus himself initiated it:

> While they were eating, Jesus took bread, said the
> blessing, broke it, and giving it to his disciples said,
> "Take and eat; this is my body." Then he took a cup,
> gave thanks, and gave it to them, saying, "Drink from
> it, all of you, for this is my blood of the covenant, which
> will be shed on behalf of many for the forgiveness of
> sins" (Matthew 26:26–28).

Jesus and his disciples were celebrating the Passover meal, according to most Gospel accounts, but the earliest Christians were satisfied with a simple meal for the setting of their Eucharist...well, perhaps some weren't satisfied with such simplicity. In a very harshly worded letter to the community he had founded at Corinth, St. Paul reprimands the Christians for their gatherings, which he said were "doing more harm than good" (1 Corinthians 11:17). These folks were apparently allowing divisions between the "haves" and "have nots" to manifest in the celebration; some would indulge in a generous meal, even getting drunk, while others were left to look on, hungry. St. Paul admonishes the community, then patiently repeats the institution narrative (the passages of the Gospels, such as that from Matthew above, which recount Christ's establishment of the Eucharist), so they might listen, relearn, repent, and reconcile.

To keep such potential and real abuses from co-opting the Eucharist, and to prevent confusion between the Christian celebration and pagan ritual meals, quickly the Eucharist was separated from a meal. However, it was usually based on those actions of Christ at the Last Supper: taking, blessing (giving thanks for), breaking and sharing of the bread, and similarly taking, blessing, and sharing the wine. Over time, these actions became the core of a more elaborate set of rites, and the Liturgy of the Eucharist as we know it took shape. It is to this complex of rites—this "second half" of Mass—that we now turn our attention.

Anamnesis vs. Reenactment

Before we do so, a few words are needed about what we are *not* doing in the Liturgy of the Eucharist. Christ's command was clear: to do this meal in his memory. In the Catholic tradition, we take care to follow these instructions closely, always checking our actions against those of Christ and his earliest followers. In fact, *The GIRM* says the Church has arranged the Liturgy of the Eucharist precisely in accordance with the words and actions of Jesus at the Last Supper: taking, blessing, breaking, sharing.[85] But we must acknowledge that, neither on Sundays nor at the annual Triduum commemoration of the passion, death, and resurrection of Christ, do we attempt to *reenact* these events of our salvation. Don't get me wrong: We certainly do believe that, in our rituals, Christ's paschal mystery is made present here and now. But it is mystery—not history—that we celebrate in the Mass. We leave reenactment to the Civil War or American Revolution buffs with their staged battles and authentic costumes, where the emphasis is on details, accuracy, and experiencing what it was like "back then." In liturgy, we do not look for such an experience. Instead, we look to experience God in our world today: to bring him glory in our own day and age, and to have our modern lives made holy by his timeless grace.

There is a word in our tradition that helps explain what we *are* doing as we "do this" in memory of Christ: *anamnesis*. This Greek word is the name of an important component of the Eucharistic Prayer, which I will describe in more detail later in the chapter. The word also represents a key characteristic of Christian worship as a whole and helps differentiate our actions in the Liturgy of the Eucharist from mere reenactment. Frank Senn says *anamnesis* is practically untranslatable into English, and the usual attempts—"commemoration," "remembrance," etc.— are all too firmly rooted in the past.[86] *Anamnesis* is more than mere recollection. Senn says it means something more like *reactualization*, in that it suggests an event, person, or thing from the past actually becomes a *present* event, person, or thing. It means we are *making present* now some reality from long ago.

Senn goes on to say that such a memorial in Jewish thought meant recalling something to God, such as a person or a promise. This may seem odd, as we don't think of God as particularly forgetful, but reminding God about a particular promise or person is something we do more for our sake than for God's.

In the context of the Eucharist, what we are recalling to God is the sacrifice of Jesus Christ, and the reason we recall this to God is so that the benefits of Christ's sacrifice (for example, the redemption of the world) may be available to us now, as they were to our ancestors. In a sense it is a way of professing to God our ardent belief that we are a people he has redeemed through his Christ, in his Spirit. Think of *anamnesis* as related to the word "amnesia," which we use to describe people who have forgotten who they are. Then remember that *anamnesis* begins with the negating prefix "*an-*," as in "not." Then think of what we are doing in the Liturgy of the Eucharist as standing before God, asking him never to forget who we are, who we have become, and are still becoming in Christ Jesus, his Son. In so doing, we also remind ourselves who (and whose) we are. And who are we? We are a blessed and redeemed people, "a chosen race, a royal priesthood, a holy nation," called "out of darkness into his wonderful light" (1 Peter 2:9), all because of the paschal mystery of Jesus Christ.

THE STRUCTURE OF THE LITURGY OF THE EUCHARIST

The Preparation of the Altar and Gifts

The first set of rites within the Liturgy of the Eucharist is preparatory. Lawrence Johnson says its purpose is threefold: to prepare the altar, the gifts to be offered upon it, and the faithful for the eucharistic celebration.[87] The presider prepares himself by these rites as well. In many ways, the preparation of the altar and gifts makes a connection between the ordinary things of our world and the sublime holiness of heaven. Through the presentation of gifts and careful preparation of the altar, we ritualize this connection between the ordinary and the extraordinary, and this helps prepare us for the Eucharist we are about to receive.

Before we go further, let's say more about the significance of the altar in the context of the Mass. Earlier we said the ambo is a focal point of the Liturgy of the Word. The altar is the focal point of the Liturgy of the Eucharist and could arguably be considered the most prominent liturgical furnishing of the whole Mass. Paragraphs 296–308 of *The GIRM* address the altar, the significance of which invites many regulations and directives so as to preserve its dignity and importance to the community's worship. The altar is the place on which the sacrifice of Christ is perpetuated, and it is the liturgy's strongest inanimate symbol of Christ, who Scripture calls the "living stone...precious in the sight of God" (1 Peter 2:4) and the "capstone" (Ephesians 2:20) or cornerstone of our faith. This is why altars are preferably built of stone and freestanding yet fixed to the floor, though movable altars of wood are permissible as circumstances require. The altar should be aesthetically worthy, for, as the U.S. Catholic Bishops' directive on church architecture says, "its composition should reflect the nobility, beauty, strength, and simplicity of the One it represents."[88] Because of the symbolic importance of the altar, the preparation of the altar, although it is necessarily a practical, functional rite, also possesses spiritual significance. On the practical side, the table is set for the meal that will soon take place. *The GIRM* says the altar is made ready for the Eucharist "when on it are placed the corporal, purificator, missal,"[89] and of course the eucharistic vessels. (The corporal is a square, white linen cloth upon which the vessels sit during the consecration, and a purificator is a fine, linen napkin used to catch any drips of consecrated wine.) Usually the presider and the deacon (if one is present) lead these preparations with help from the servers, arranging the items reverently but purposefully. And since the altar is an important symbol of Christ, "the cornerstone" in the worship space as it is prepared for Mass, images of the preparations Christ underwent before his passion and death come to mind: how he was anointed by a woman with expensive perfumed oil, how soldiers dressed him in special garments and a crown of thorns to mock him, how he was made to carry his own cross of execution. But Christ was also prepared for his resurrection, even if those who prepared him did so unknowingly; Joseph of Arimathea carried his body from the cross, respectfully wrapped it in clean linen, and laid it in a new tomb, while the Marys kept watch. Images of both death and resurrection surface during the preparation of the altar, that stone upon which these saving mysteries are perpetuated by Christ's body, the Church. This is an example of how the preparation of the altar connects the material and spiritual realms, preparing us for the eucharistic meal, which joins heaven to earth.

When these initial preparations are ready, the "gifts" of bread and wine are brought forth by the faithful in the third procession of the Mass. Processing the bread and wine through the worship space to the altar establishes a few important realities: First, it draws attention to the gifts themselves, which are earthly things made by human hands. As Jesus took such earthly things in his hands at the Last Supper, so bread and wine are presented to the presider, who receives them before all.

Communities may desire to add objects to this procession to express what is important to them on special occasions like first Communions, weddings, etc. However, it is preferable that additional objects *not* be added to the gifts procession, for this practice dilutes the symbolic force of the bread and wine: a force that comes, ironically, from their simplicity. However, *The GIRM* says it is acceptable that gifts for the poor be included in this procession,[90] but the bread and wine should be more prominent.

Secondly, the procession and presentation of the gifts expresses the desire of the faithful to be a real part of the eucharistic sacrifice. It was a very ancient practice in the Church for the faithful to bring the gifts of bread and wine to the celebration from among their own stores, made by their own hands, thus personalizing their participation in the Eucharist even more. This sign of the faithful's personal investment in the mystery to be celebrated is preserved today by their procession and presentation of the gifts.

In yet another layer of symbolism, the gifts procession points to the Communion procession to come. In the first, earthly gifts are humbly presented; in the second, heavenly gifts are humbly received.

As the presider receives the gifts, he says prayers praising God for these good fruits of creation. As he receives the vessel of wine, he pours a bit of water into it: an ancient symbol of Christ's union with us. The wine stands for Christ's blood and the water for the Church. The presider says a quiet prayer as he does this, which summarizes this reality, then he says the prayer of thanksgiving for the wine, which parallels that said for the bread. To the prayer over each gift, if the prayers are said audibly, the assembly responds with the acclamation, "Blessed be God for ever."[91]

After this the presider bows profoundly and says inaudibly a prayer that the sacrifice we are about to offer be, in its humility, pleasing to God. This is a medieval prayer with scriptural roots in the Book of Daniel.[92]

Then, if incense is used at that Mass, he incenses the gifts, the altar, and the cross, "so as to signify the Church's offering and prayer rising like incense in the sight of God."[93] Then a server or the deacon takes the thurible (which holds the incense) from the presider and incenses the priest himself, then the people, as a sign of their dignity in Christ, by virtue of their baptism. The assembly receives this sign of their holiness by making a profound bow.

The last of the physical preparations then takes place: the washing of hands. The priest washes his hands in a bowl of water and dries them, while praying, inaudibly, a verse from Psalm

51 that he be cleansed from sinfulness. This ancient rite recalls the Jewish roots of Christian prayer; ritual washing was a common element of ancient Jewish liturgical culture.

Song for the Preparation of the Altar and Gifts

On Sundays, music accompanies the procession and presentation of the gifts, as well as the preparations of the altar and the prayers of the priest. (This is why at most Sunday Masses you do not hear the above-mentioned prayers of the priest, though some are said inaudibly even when there is no music.) The song accompanying the preparation of the altar and gifts can be sung by all or by the choir alone. It could even be an instrumental piece, and sometimes this is the best choice for a simpler celebration. The purpose of the music here is the same as at the entrance procession: to begin the Liturgy of the Eucharist, to foster the unity of those gathered and to turn their minds and hearts to the particular aspects of the mystery about to be celebrated, and finally to accompany the actions that are taking place, namely the procession of the gifts, their presentation, and the preparations at the altar.[94]

This last function is not to be forgotten—the music is meant to accompany the actions taking place. *The GIRM* says the music should last at least until the gifts are placed on the altar. The rites become awkward when the music "runs out" before this; a musical void lends a rushed quality to the remaining preparations. It is more desirable that the song be slightly longer than needed rather than end precipitously before the rites are finished. Ideally, music directors and accompanists should be watchful during this rite and plan the music's end to correspond as closely as possible with the washing of hands.

There is one last rite in this first of three main parts of the Liturgy of the Eucharist: the Prayer over the Offerings and its Invitation. With their sacrificial imagery, these prayer texts ready us for the Eucharistic Prayer that follows. The presider invites the people to pray, and their response articulates the overarching purpose of our worship: that the sacrifice be acceptable for God's glory and for the good of the Church, both local and universal. After this response, the presider pronounces the Prayer over the Offerings. The texts for this prayer vary, but all ask God to accept the offerings at hand and express the gathered community's desire to be one with the offering.[95] This desire expressed, all is ready for the heart and soul of the Mass: the Eucharistic Prayer.

The Eucharistic Prayer and Its Acclamations

Characteristics of the Eucharistic Prayer

The word "eucharist" comes from a Greek word meaning "thanksgiving," and the Eucharistic Prayer is the great thanksgiving of the people, together with the priestly presider, to God. It is often said that the Eucharistic Prayer is the heart of the Mass, because, more than any other part of the Mass, it contains that which Christ himself asked us to do in his memory. Together with the reception of holy Communion by the faithful, to which the Eucharistic Prayer is inextricably linked, it is the high point in the Mass. And since the sacrament of the Eucharist is the greatest of all the sacraments of the Christian life, one could say that the Eucharistic Prayer and the reception of holy Communion together bring us to the heart of the Christian life itself.

The prayer is Trinitarian in structure yet has very Jewish roots. (The prayer Jesus prayed over the gifts at the Last Supper was a clear—if extraordinary—example of Jewish table prayer.) It is a prayer addressed, almost entirely, to God the Father, whose generosity toward creation is greatly praised. Then, still addressing God, the prayer remembers and praises the accomplishments of Jesus Christ, particularly his paschal mystery, in the *anamnetic* sense of remembering, which begs God to make present the saving work of the Son for the benefit of the gathered community here and now. Finally, the prayer asks God to send the Holy Spirit upon both the bread and wine and upon those who will partake of them. It closes with a Trinitarian doxology, or short acclamation giving glory to God, through Christ, in union with the Holy Spirit. The Eucharistic Prayer's clear structure of invocation, *anamnesis,* and petition marks it as the Christian descendant of Jewish *Berakah* prayers of blessing and thanksgiving to God.

In the Eastern Christian Churches the Eucharistic Prayer is known as the *Anaphora*, a name that means offering. This understanding of the prayer as offering holds true in the Western, Roman Church as well, though we give the prayer a different name. The assembly, led by the priest, offers the bread and wine, recalling the redemptive offering of Jesus Christ on the cross. As John Barry Ryan states, in so doing the assembly expresses its desire to become part of the once-for-all offering of Christ, becoming, through both the prayer and through the meal that follows, the body of Christ, broken and shared.[96]

Ryan also says the prayer, in its various versions, has a theme of reconciliation. The entire prayer is one of thanksgiving for the reconciliation of humans to God in the paschal mystery of Christ. But the implications of this reconciliation for the human race, for the living to the dead, for heaven to earth, are clearly articulated in the prayer. Again, the link between the Eucharistic Prayer and the Communion meal, which makes us one with Christ and with each other, draws out and deepens the Eucharistic Prayer's character of reconciliation.

This sums up the overarching characteristics of the prayer. However, as the core rite of the Mass, the Eucharistic Prayer's component parts merit a closer look. Before we examine them, however, let's set out a few practical points about the Eucharistic Prayer—or perhaps I should say Eucharistic *Prayers*, for there is more than one! Although as a rule only one of these great prayers of thanksgiving is pronounced at each Mass, there are four versions of the Eucharistic Prayer for general use, two more for Masses of reconciliation, a Eucharistic Prayer for various particular needs and special occasions, and three more for use with children (though not all of these Eucharistic Prayers have been retranslated according to the new norms for translation used to produce the Third Edition of *The Roman Missal*; for more information on these new norms, see the Appendix). For centuries Eucharistic Prayer I (also known as the Roman Canon) was the only Eucharistic Prayer used in the Roman Church, but after the Second Vatican Council, new prayers were composed based closely on ancient Eastern *anaphoras* and patristic (authoritative, early-Church) sources. These additional Eucharistic Prayers are yet another gift of the council and the scholarship that followed it, and add variety and depth to the liturgical life of Catholics.

The Parts of the Eucharistic Prayer

The Eucharistic Prayer begins with the preface, and though its text varies, it always begins with the same ancient dialogue we have already heard twice in the Mass, acknowledging the presence of the Lord in both assembly and presider. Then the assembly is encouraged to "lift" their hearts up to the Lord, and they respond affirming this command. The original Latin text seems awkward; a truly literal translation would have it as, "Up hearts!" and "We have, to the Lord," which makes scholars think it was originally one sentence, divided to create a dialogue, not unlike a chant at a sporting event.[97]

The priest then invites the assembly to give thanks and praise, and the assembly again affirms this invitation. The preface prayer goes on to give God praise and thanks for the paschal mystery of his Son, getting more specific in its praise in accord with the particular season, feast, or occasion. More than eighty different prefaces have been composed for use with the various Eucharistic Prayers. Lawrence Johnson reflects that the preface sets the tone for the praise and thanksgiving that threads through the whole Eucharistic Prayer and helps unite priest and people, who together offer this great thanksgiving to God.[98]

Next is the acclamation known as the "*Sanctus*" or "Holy, Holy, Holy," which the end of the preface introduces with imagery of heavenly choirs of angels. The text of the *Sanctus* comes from the prophet Isaiah and the Gospel of Matthew. The *Sanctus* is not a "singing break"—*The GIRM* is clear that the *Sanctus* constitutes part of the Eucharistic Prayer itself.[99] In the *Sanctus*, heaven and earth, the living and those who have gone before us in death, are joined in singing God's praises. To preserve the festivity of this important acclamation, it should be sung whenever possible, even if instrumental accompaniment is not available. The priest and people are perfectly capable of singing this song of praise without accompaniment, knowing all the angels and saints are singing with them!

A rite called the Epiclesis, a word that means "invoking" or "calling," comes next. In it, the presider calls upon the Holy Spirit to sanctify the gifts of bread and wine, and the people who will partake of them. His hand gestures (arms extended, then brought together over the gifts, making the Sign of the Cross), both illustrate and effect this invocation. The Holy Spirit is not mentioned explicitly in the Epiclesis of Eucharistic Prayer I (the Roman Canon), but the other Eucharistic Prayers make clear what the Roman Canon merely implies: that the job of sanctification, in this and all cases, falls to that third member of the Holy Trinity.

What is the descent of the Holy Spirit like? Eucharistic Prayer II gives us a powerful image: the Holy Spirit like dew. This image invites the imagination to ponder this natural phenomenon, which falls in the early morning, soaking everything just enough to make the grass glow green, to refresh flowers before the morning sun, to wash the world and make it new again each day. It also invokes images of the Hebrews in the Book of Exodus, wandering in exile after their miraculous escape from slavery, when God fed them with bread from heaven, which fell to earth in the night like dew. This imagery assures us that the Holy Spirit's constant presence, nourishment, and refreshment will bless us in the Eucharist.

If the Eucharistic Prayer is the heart of the Mass, then the institution narrative, which comes next, is the heart of hearts. In the context of a prayer to God the Father, the words of Jesus at the Last Supper are retold, and these ancient words give power and efficacy to the words of the presider, which merely echo those of Christ. Many Catholics think of this part of the Eucharistic Prayer as the one that "counts," for example, as the moment of consecration, when bread and wine become Body and Blood. While it is accurate to say these words are consecratory (*The GIRM* calls this the rite by which the sacrifice of the Mass is effected[100]), modern scholarship emphasizes the integrity and completeness of the whole Eucharistic Prayer; singling out some parts as "counting" more than others may take away from our appreciation for the consecratory power of the prayer as a whole. That said, the institution narrative and the elevation of the Body and Blood are moments to which the faithful rightly respond with profound silence and undivided attention, for in our very midst, God transforms mundane things of our world into the gift of himself for our salvation.

After the words of institution, the presider introduces the Mystery of Faith or Memorial Acclamation. This acclamation, sung by all, sums up and praises the paschal mystery of Christ, linking the celebration at hand to the whole of salvation history. There is a choice of three different texts for it; it is usually up to the music director to decide which is used at a given Mass. By this sung acclamation and the *Anamnesis* prayer that follows, the Church fulfills Christ's command to perpetuate his death and resurrection in the Eucharist.[101] It is noteworthy that, unlike the rest of the Eucharistic Prayer which is addressed to God the Father, each version of the Mystery of Faith addresses Christ the Son, who is now sacramentally present on the altar.

After this short song comes the *Anamnesis*. We have talked about the *anamnetic* character of the Mass itself, and especially the Liturgy of the Eucharist; more than merely "remembering" Christ's sacrifice, the thanksgiving we offer, through God's grace, makes the paschal mystery present here and now, so that we may share, with our ancestors in faith, its saving effects. The *Anamnesis* articulates this reality and places it alongside the offering of real food and drink through the Holy Spirit as a sacrifice of praise. Thus the oblation follows quickly on the heels of the *Anamnesis*, making this strong connection between the sacrifice at hand and the sacrifice that gives it power: Christ's, made once and for all. *The GIRM*, referencing the Constitution on the Sacred Liturgy, beautifully sums up the meaning of the oblation:

> The Church's intention, indeed, is that the faithful not only offer this unblemished sacrificial Victim but also learn to offer their very selves, and so day by day to be brought, through the mediation of Christ, into unity with God and with each other, so that God may at last be all in all.[102]

In all the Eucharistic Prayers except the Roman Canon, a "second" or "Communion" Epiclesis follows the oblation. This second invocation of the Holy Spirit is brief, and its subject is not the gifts on the altar but the faithful who will partake of them. Specifically, it prays that unity will be the fruit of the meal for those who partake of it. This second Epiclesis is a strong reminder that it is not merely the bread and wine that are transformed in the eucharistic act, but the body of Christ as well.

Prayers of intercession follow, "by which expression is given to the fact that the Eucharist is celebrated in communion with the whole Church, of both heaven and of earth." [103] The gathered assembly looks far beyond itself in these intercessions, not unlike in the General Intercessions that conclude the Liturgy of the Word. But more than praying for the Church universal, in these intercessions the community acknowledges that it celebrates the Eucharist here and now in union with the whole communion of saints: that great band of believers, living and dead, who form the body of Christ. These intercessions remind us that we are on a journey and keep us connected to those ahead of us on the road home. With Mary and all the saints, the faithful departed await us at the heavenly banquet, prefigured by our celebration of the Eucharist.

Finally we come to the Doxology, which praises the Father, through the Son with the Holy Spirit, and which, with the Great Amen, concludes the Eucharistic Prayer. The presider lifts the bread and wine high in one final gesture of offering and chants the Doxology. Then the people, in an "Amen" more heartfelt and profound than any yet, make this great prayer of thanksgiving their own, pledging themselves as one to a life of gratitude for God's gifts, especially the paschal mystery of his Son. For this is what "Amen" truly means; not just "I believe, I agree," but "I promise, I pledge." The "Great Amen" is sung whenever possible, for singing lends the solemnity this liturgical moment needs. It is a highly important and thus participative acclamation; even if you are not given to much singing, sing this! "Amen, Amen," our sacrifice of praise is complete!

The Communion Rite

Mass continues to peak with the rites that follow: those of final preparation and distribution of holy Communion. These rites are marked by themes of unity and peace; they help spiritually prepare us to receive the Lord. In the Communion Rite our belief that the Eucharist unites us not just with Christ but with one another is made clear.

The first way this spiritual Communion is expressed is through the recitation of the Lord's Prayer (or as Catholics like to call it, the Our Father). The presider invites the people to pray, and all join in this well-known, ancient, and most authoritative prayer. In doing so, we share a common posture of standing, owning our dignity as brothers and sisters of Christ. (In some parishes people hold hands; in others, each holds his hands outstretched. Neither is wrong, but neither is called for by *The GIRM*, which simply indicates that all should stand after the Great Amen.[104]) We pronounce the words Jesus himself taught us, and know in saying them, we are one with one another, with Christians around the world (of every denomination!), and with all who have come before us. Before the prayer ends with a doxology said by all, the presider alone adds an additional petition for peace and deliverance from evil. This insertion, called the embolism, is a very ancient part of the Lord's Prayer in the Catholic tradition. (It can also be a great source of embarrassment to visiting Protestants, who, not expecting it, sometimes keep praying by themselves!)

To heighten the solemn unity of this moment, the Lord's Prayer may be sung, as long as the musical setting is well-known so no one is left out (what a sad irony that would be!). Some parishes so enjoy singing the Lord's Prayer that they do so each week, across all seasons. In doing so they miss an opportunity to vary the level of solemnity in the liturgy as a whole: a principle known as progressive solemnity. The principle of progressive solemnity holds that not every Sunday of the Church year (for instance, the 22nd Sunday in ordinary time) is as important as every other (for example, the Solemnity of Our Lord Christ the King), and the parts we choose to sing or not sing, the festivity of our décor, the complexity of our processions, etc., all help differentiate the varying levels of festivity that make our worship tradition so rich. The Lord's Prayer is one of those rites we may choose to sing or not sing at any given Mass, but when it is sung, the celebration seems extra special.

After the Lord's Prayer, the faithful exchange a sign of peace at the presider's invitation. In Jesus' Sermon on the Mount from the Gospel of Matthew, he urged his followers to be at peace with one another before making an offering to the Lord. Christians interpreted this as a command to reconcile their differences before receiving the Body and Blood of the Lord in Communion: the ultimate sign of unity, not to be taken in vain. Remember that Christians in the earliest Church did not merely see each other on Sundays but lived communally to support each other's physical, social, and financial needs; the Acts of the Apostles describes such Christian communities who shared all things in common. If you've ever been thrown together with a roommate, such as in college or at camp, you know living with someone—even a brother, sister, or spouse!—can be challenging. Petty (and not-so-petty) disagreements can sour even the closest of relationships. The sign or kiss of peace finds a place in the Communion Rite so we may forgive and be forgiven before receiving the Lord in Communion.

Desiring forgiveness and reconciliation with our fellow humans, we turn to those around us with a tangible greeting of peace, a handshake, perhaps a brief embrace. It is not the time for small talk, compliments, or other niceties, and it should certainly not go on and on, becoming "recess" in the middle of Mass (I have seen this happen; perhaps it is why *The GIRM* recommends the sign of peace be conducted with sobriety![105]). The sign of peace is nothing more or less than a physical acknowledgment that the peace in which Christ calls us to live is not simply an idea. It means getting along with one another in big and small ways. It means forgiving one another over and over. It is interesting to note that for centuries the sign of peace occurred after the Prayer of the Faithful, or in the ancient Church, at the very start of Mass. It was moved to its present position before Communion, presumably to show the connection between Eucharist and the peace and joy that come from true friendship, in Christ, with one another.

The breaking of the bread is next: yet another rite that symbolizes the unity of those gathered in Christ. This moment would be significant merely for its power to remind us of those founding, eucharistic actions of Christ at the Last Supper (from Matthew chapter 26: "Jesus took bread, said the blessing, broke it, and giving it to his disciples said, 'Take and eat; this is my body'"). One can hear the symbolism of this rite in St. Paul's questions to the new disciples at Corinth: "The cup of blessing that we bless, is it not a participation in the blood of Christ? The bread that we break, is it not a participation in the body of Christ?" (1 Corinthians 10:16). So the bread, though broken, is one loaf, so we who will share in this meal become "one body, one Spirit in Christ,"[106] or as St. Paul continues to the Corinthians, "because the loaf of bread is one, we, though many, are one body, for we all partake of the one loaf."

During the breaking of the bread, the presider takes a small piece of the consecrated bread and adds it to the precious blood. This early medieval rite, called the commingling, is a symbolic reuniting of Body and Blood to symbolize the resurrection of Christ, and the presider's accompanying prayer asks for the ultimate fruit of the meal: eternal life.

At this time the choir and assembly sing the Lamb of God, a litany (or call-and-response style song) that accompanies the rite at hand. Its text, from the first chapter of John's Gospel, makes the Passover connection with the bread and wine that are broken and poured at this time: Jesus is the Lamb of God, the spotless victim who takes away the world's sins, freeing God's people from slavery to sin and death. This banquet is our eternal Passover. The choir and assembly sing the Lamb of God until the ritual action is complete, repeating the first line as many times as is necessary, and ending with a plea for peace.

Next both presider and people prepare themselves, finally, for Communion. The priest says a prayer inaudibly, asking for forgiveness of sins while the people silently pray. Then, elevating the Body and Blood, the presiding priest invites the people to "behold" the Lamb of God, which evokes scenes from Jesus' passion and reminds them of their blessedness in being called to this banquet. The people respond with a line paraphrased from Scripture: "Lord, I am not worthy that you should enter under my roof, but only say the word and my soul shall be healed."[107] Huh? We may not catch this reference to the story of the faithful centurion in Matthew's Gospel, whom the Lord promised to accompany to the centurion's home to heal his beloved servant. Even if we do, it's a bit strange. Do we mean the roofs of our mouths? Now that *would* be strange. Certainly not! The deep symbolism of the moment reminds us that our bodies are the homes of our souls, and both are given to us by the Lord. In eating and drinking at the Lord's table, we invite the Lord into our lives, our selves, our homes. We open ourselves to his grace, his mercy, and his love. His love is not merited by us but given freely anyway, despite our sins. And—thank God!—it is a love with the power to make us whole again.

As the presider consumes the bread and wine, the Communion Song begins. This song accompanies the faithful's reception of Communion and so should last for the duration of the procession at least. (Sometimes two or more songs are needed.) The faithful are invited to sing along with this song. To encourage them to do so, the song should be well-known and memorable so that they may sing it without the aid of a hymnal (since they will be processing to Communion). As for the subject matter of the Communion Song, there are many options. Music directors could find (or compose) a setting of the proper Communion Antiphon from the *Roman Gradual*. *Sing to the Lord* suggests that themes of "joy, wonder, unity, gratitude, and praise," or themes that capture the subject matter of the day's Gospel reading are all appropriate.[108] Those responsible for choosing the music at Mass should remember what *The GIRM* names as the purpose of the Communion

Song: "to express the spiritual union of the communicants by means of the unity of their voices, to show gladness of heart, and to bring out more clearly the 'communitarian' character of the procession to receive the Eucharist."[109] Because of these aims, although instrumental music or choir pieces are permitted at Communion, *Sing to the Lord* calls communal singing in this moment "commendable." [110]

All the while, the faithful are gracefully going to the table, prayerfully processing to receive Christ in bread and wine. This is the only procession in the Mass in which nearly everyone takes part, and the symbolism of the act is heightened by its participatory nature. We walk together to God, who gives us food for our continued journey.

The actual reception of Communion is a simple rite; a person approaches the presider, deacon, or lay minister, who raises the host, makes eye contact, and says, "the body of Christ." The other responds, "Amen." There is no need for additional words to be added or individual names to be used, such as "Jane, the body of Christ," because this takes away from the true reality of the moment. In saying only, "the body of Christ," the minister is saying that person's name, in the truest sense. We die to our own selves in this paschal meal, and we rise again as one body in Christ. This is not to say Christians are conformists who don't want people to be themselves; it is to say that our own, unique, beautiful selves are made perfect—made what God meant us to be—in Christ, through the Eucharist. This is what St. Augustine meant when he said,

> …it's the mystery meaning you that has been placed on the Lord's table; what you receive is the mystery that means you. It is to what you are that you reply Amen, and by so replying you express your assent. What you hear, you see, is The body of Christ, and you answer, Amen. So be a member of the body of Christ, in order to make that Amen true.[111]

One note that treads on a sometimes painful subject: Who receives Communion in the Catholic Church? The answer is: Catholics only. This "closed" policy on the Eucharist is different from many other Christian denominations and may seem very unwelcoming. Sometimes it helps assuage hurt feelings to explain why Communion in the Catholic Church is only open to Catholics. In the Catholic tradition, holy Communion is one of three Rites of Initiation into the faith. (The others are baptism and confirmation.) To receive the Eucharist in our tradition is, among other things, to declare your intention to hold and keep the Catholic faith as your own. If one is not willing or ready to make such a profession and commitment, one should abstain from receiving those sacraments of membership that signify it. (By contrast, marriage is not a sacrament of initiation, so a non-Catholic may marry a Catholic in a Catholic wedding, but this act does not signify the non-Catholic's desire, necessarily, to join the Church.) This is why Communion in the Catholic Church is only open to Catholics.

When the Communion procession is complete and the vessels used at the meal have been purified (cleansed by the priest, deacon, or an acolyte of any traces of the precious Body and Blood) and set reverently aside, and when any leftover consecrated hosts have been returned to the tabernacle with holy dispatch, then all are seated for a moment (or two) of prayerful silence. *The GIRM* calls this a "sacred silence," and it will be that if enough time is permitted for the silence to "soak in." Remembering what was said about the importance of silence in the last chapter, this moment is also an important time for those gathered to spiritually process what has just taken place. Without it, Eucharist may seem like just another in the relentless progression of events that mark the passing of time in secular culture. (Mass: check! Now on to lunch....)

An alternative *The GIRM* offers in this moment—one that provides space for a more directed, communal reflection on the Eucharist—is for the assembly to sing together a hymn or psalm of praise. Typically all stand and sing, which encourages participation, and the song is one of joy and praise to God for what has been given to us in Christ. This Hymn of Praise after Communion is a festive liturgical option that is best employed to mark a particularly joyful season such as Christmas or Easter. To use this option each week may deprive the assembly of much-needed time to silently reflect on the gift of Christ in the Eucharist.

Finally comes the prayer after Communion. The presider invites all to pray, and a brief silence is observed (it can be very brief if an extended silence came right before). This prayer's text varies from Sunday to Sunday, from feast to feast, but the substance of the prayer is always to ask, as *The GIRM* puts it, "for the fruits of the mystery just celebrated." [112] The prayer after Communion asks God to make us, through the meal we have shared, a eucharistic people in the world.

This prayer provides an excellent conclusion to the Communion Rite because it makes a transition from celebration to mission. In the next chapter we will explore the Concluding Rite of Mass and discover how, in it, we are effectively sent into the service of the Lord.

DISCUSSION QUESTIONS

1. *What is* anamnesis? *Why is* anamnesis *a better concept than "reenactment" in thinking about what happens during the Liturgy of the Eucharist?*

2. *What is the significance of the altar in Catholic worship? Why do you think altars carry so much importance in the Catholic tradition?*

3. *Why is the Eucharistic Prayer often called "the heart of the Mass?" What makes it so? Is it the heart of your experience of Mass? Why or why not?*

4. *Which particular part of the Eucharistic Prayer was the most interesting or unexpected to you? Why?*

5. *What is the principle of progressive solemnity, and how does it affect the choices of those responsible for preparing the liturgy?*

6. *Have you experienced the practice of singing a hymn of praise after Communion? What was the experience like?*

CHAPTER 7

The Concluding Rite:
Liturgy and Life

In less than 100 words, *The GIRM* describes in detail the structure of the Concluding Rite of Mass. *The GIRM* may be brief on this subject because the Concluding Rite itself is quite brief. It begins with an optional opportunity for the community's announcements, if any are necessary, then proceeds to the final liturgical greeting of the Mass: "The Lord be with you./ And with your spirit."[113] A blessing or prayer follows, in shorter or longer form, then the people are dismissed by the deacon (if present) or presider, using one of a few formulas. The people respond giving thanks, and that's it. The end. As the ministers process out of the worship space, the faithful often sing a song or hymn, but no such song is called for by *The GIRM*.

Why such an abrupt, insignificant-seeming ending to such a holy, profound celebration? Perhaps it only seems insignificant. Taking a closer look at the component parts of the Concluding Rite reveals it as the bridge over which the Catholic faith, especially its expression in Mass, travels into the daily lives of Catholics and into the world outside church walls.

THE STRUCTURE OF THE CONCLUDING RITE

Like every other time it is used in the Mass, the liturgical greeting between presider and assembly signals a shift in the celebration. It focuses our minds and hearts on something new.[114] Fr. Gerald T. Chinchar says the something new, in this case the Concluding Rite of Mass, is not just a perfunctory dismissal: as in, "we have all these people here at Mass, and somehow we've got to get them to go home, so let's have a dismissal." Rather, Chinchar says the Concluding Rite connects the dismissal with what has come before in our celebration, creating a purposeful going forth to conclude the Mass.

And what has come before? In an immediate sense the prayer after Communion has come before, if there were no announcements. With its summary character and focus on the eucharistic meal's power for our daily lives, the prayer after Communion invited the assembly to consider "life after Mass": a new life, a changed life, nourished at the banquet of the Lord. If the community's announcements came immediately before, they too—though they carry no ritual or theological significance, and occur only if they are necessary—may, as a happy side effect, remind the faithful that there is work to be done as we go forth from the table.

In a broader sense, what has come before the Concluding Rite is the purest expression of our faith: the liturgy, that "source and summit" of our lives as Christians. In the Introductory Rites we are gathered as one and reoriented to the life of God. In the Liturgy of the Word we hear, reflect on, and respond to God's mighty Word—a word of peace, of justice, of love, of friendship between humans and God and among one another. By it we are moved to offer petitions, not just for ourselves but for all. In the Liturgy of the Eucharist we are completely incorporated into the body of God's Word, Jesus Christ. We eat his flesh and drink his blood, and his story becomes our story, too. His suffering and death are now ours, and so is his resurrection.

From this intense experience of worship, the Concluding Rite of Mass purposefully sends us forth. It sends us forth not as we were, but as we are now: as the body of Christ. Recall the third aspect of the word "mystery" in the phrase "paschal mystery" (that is, the heart and soul of what we celebrate at Mass, discussed in chapter 3). It refers to the mystery of the Church:

the sacramental and ritual life of believers. But our sacramental and ritual life is not all we are, even if it is our spiritual and moral center. The sacraments keep us in motion as a pilgrim people. The Eucharist in particular keeps the body of Christ nourished to be Christ and continually molds us in his image. Yes, we become Christ through this meal, but this is not enough; we must be Christ in the world. The Concluding Rite of Mass dismisses us to live the paschal mystery of Christ in the world.

Both forms of the blessing that follow the liturgical greeting point up this invitation to paschal mystery living. The simple form is Trinitarian, blessing the faithful in the name of the Father, Son, and Holy Spirit. As this blessing is given, the faithful are invited to make the Sign of the Cross, as they did at the start of Mass. As we gather in the name of the Three-in-One, so too do we go forth. Fr. Kevin Seasoltz says people formed by the liturgy are a Trinitarian people with a distinctive identity, for we are made in the image of a mysteriously relational God.[115] As God is both one and three, so the liturgy calls and sends us forth to be one, though many. We are created to be like our Creator: that is, not simply to have relationships but to *be* the relationships we have. This is what it means, after all, to be one body. We live for one another.

The solemn blessing is an option the presider may use instead of the simple blessing and is especially appropriate on more festive occasions. It often takes the form of a four-part blessing, and to each part the assembly responds, "Amen." Chinchar says, more than the simple blessing, the solemn blessing gives expression to the connections between the paschal mystery we celebrate in Mass and the paschal mystery living that the Mass calls us to do in the world.[116] In addition, the solemn blessings remind us of the eternal reward that awaits us at the end of our paschal pilgrimage through life. For example, the fourth blessing designated for use in ordinary time asks that God "order" our days in his peace, so that "on this life's journey," we may be "effective in good works, rich in the gifts of hope, faith, and charity, and may come happily to eternal life."[117] Similarly, the solemn blessing for the Feast of Epiphany asks that, just as God has appeared as a light to all nations on this great feast, we too may be a light to our sisters and brothers. "And so when [our] pilgrimage is ended," it concludes, "may [we] come to him whom the Magi sought as they followed the star and whom they found with great joy, the Light from Light, who is Christ the Lord."[118]

A third option, besides the simple or solemn blessing, is for the presider to say or chant a special prayer over the people. He (or the deacon if one is present) invites the assembly to bow their heads. The presiding priest then says the prayer over the people, a short prayer of blessing and protection, addressed directly to God, through Christ. The people then respond, "Amen." There are twenty-eight different prayers over the people in *The Roman Missal*, addressing various particular needs and desires for the faithful, and as they are less solemn, the presider can choose to use one at any Mass.

The very last element of the Mass is the dismissal. Like the Concluding Rite as a whole, the dismissal appears simple, straightforward, and functional, and it is. The presider (or deacon if one is present) says one of four possible phrases of dismissal to the assembly, who respond in thanksgiving. After this the presider venerates the altar with a kiss and, with the other ministers, leaves the worship space.

A closer look at the dismissal language reveals it as a bold emblem of the whole worship experience and its life-directing impact on those who celebrate it. The original Latin text (*Ite, missa est*) contains the word *missa*, which basically means "dismissal" but has connotations of "being sent," which imply the "mission" (a similarly derived word) of those who dine at the eucharistic table: to be the body of Christ in the world by doing Christ's work. Most English textual options for the dismissal point up well these kingdom-building connotations inherent in the original Latin, like option B: "Go and announce the Gospel of the Lord," and especially option C: "Go in peace, glorifying the Lord by your life." It has been reported that Pope Benedict XVI took a personal interest in the translation and selection of the dismissal language for the new *Missal* out of a particular interest in helping the faithful make connections between the Mass and the lives they lead as Catholics in the world.[119]

And the dismissal is an emblem for the whole Mass in another, more literal way. It is interesting to note that from this dismissal word, *missa*, we derive the term "Mass." This is perhaps the best evidence of the significance, despite its brevity, of the Concluding Rite. We Catholics have named the whole of what we do in worship, the Mass, for the mission of paschal mystery living on which it sends us when it is complete.

A CONCLUDING SONG?

Many of you could be scratching your heads about now, wondering why I am speaking of the Mass' completion without discussing the concluding song. In most North American Catholic parishes, ending Mass with an uplifting hymn or song, led by the choir but usually involving the whole assembly, is standard practice. But surprisingly, this song is nowhere to be found in the ritual books. It is not mentioned in *The GIRM*, and although *Sing to the Lord* contains a short paragraph on the concluding song, it begins by saying it is not necessary.[120]

The concluding song is a tradition that developed in the early twentieth century, when active participation by the faithful was a sought-after value of worship in an increasing number of parishes. However, before the reforms of the Mass brought by Vatican II in the mid-1960s, there were limited means of achieving this participation of the faithful during Mass, which remained in a foreign language and was mostly conducted at the altar by the priest. Hymns and songs, sung by the faithful, were introduced during Mass as ways of encouraging prayerful participation by the people, and this is how a song came to be customary at the end of the Mass in some places in the world. There was also a sense in some circles that the ending of Mass, for example, the dismissal, was somewhat abrupt, and that some further element was needed to bring closure to the eucharistic liturgy. This attitude encouraged the custom of concluding Mass with a participative song.

Chinchar says this same attitude nudges us toward an insight about our worship that the concluding song may make it difficult to discern: He says the Mass ought not have closure, but rather, should open us onto life.[121] In this sense, the Mass is like the meal a marathoner eats the night before the big race or like the pep talk given to the basketball team before the state championship. Of course, unlike these examples, the celebration of the liturgy is an end in itself; in it, God is glorified and the faithful are sanctified. But sanctified for what? Not for nothing, and certainly not simply to go eat lunch! Rather, we are sanctified to *live* the Gospel, to *live* the faith, to *live* the liturgy.

Then again, perhaps a concluding song, if well-chosen and led by the music ministers, can help foster in the faithful a sense of mission. Songs whose lyrics make connections between the liturgy and the work of the body of Christ in the world seem especially appropriate. Musicians (and the faithful) should beware of songs that seem to convey that we alone go forth on mission by neglecting to mention God much or at all (take close notice of the song lyrics at Mass for a while and you will soon find an example of what I'm describing!). Well-crafted lyrics for concluding songs will rightly express that we go forth *as we are sent*, and *only through God* will we accomplish the work of building the kingdom. Unfortunately many contemporary songs fail to make plain this reality of our complete dependence on God for both our needs and for our accomplishments. At the same time, plenty of composers have written engaging lyrics that do this well. This points up again the responsibility of music directors and others who select music for Mass to go through all available resources carefully, only selecting the most theologically, musically, and poetically successful songs.

LITURGY AND LIFE

In his letter introducing the Year of the Eucharist in 2004–2005, Pope John Paul II said, "The dismissal at the end of each Mass is *a charge* given to Christians, inviting them to work for the spread of the Gospel and the imbuing of society with Christian values."[122] In the same letter, the Holy Father went on to describe the eucharistic attitude—that is, one of unfaltering gratitude, recognizing all of creation's contingency on its Creator—that results from faithful celebration of Christ's paschal mystery in the Mass. Possessing a eucharistic attitude can change not only the life of the individual, but the world, "For the Eucharist is a mode of being, which passes from Jesus into each Christian, through whose testimony it is meant to spread throughout society and culture. For this to happen, each member of the faithful must assimilate, through personal and communal meditation, the values which the Eucharist expresses, the attitudes it inspires, the resolutions to which it gives rise."[123]

What does the Holy Father mean when he speaks of "values" of the Eucharist? What, at its core, does the Eucharist *mean*? This is best answered by Jesus himself in the Gospel of John. Unlike the other three Gospels, John's account does not describe the meal among Jesus and his disciples on the night before his death. Instead, it describes Jesus doing something very strange in the middle of the meal:

> [Jesus] rose from supper and took off his outer
> garments. He took a towel and tied it around his waist.

Then he poured water into a basin and began to wash
the disciples' feet and dry them with the towel around
his waist (John 13:4–5).

John's description of this radical act of self-sacrificing service, set alongside the other Gospels' accounts of the first Eucharist, puts the meaning of the meal into sharp relief. Living
a eucharistic life—a life rooted in celebrating the sacrament of
love—means living for others.

Unfortunately, in our everyday lives it is tempting to mistake the notion of "living for others" for simply not being a
jerk, like cranky, miserly old Ebenezer Scrooge from Dickens'
A Christmas Carol. Who wants to be like that? Or we may only
ever seek out opportunities for being kind and self-sacrificing
for those who are close to us when it's convenient. Sure, I feed
the hungry every day...if my husband and child count as "the
hungry." (They don't.)

To really get at what "living for others" might mean as Jesus modeled it, let's look again at what Jesus was *doing* when
he washed the disciples' feet. This was not normal behavior for
someone like Jesus! It was not an everyday nicety, to wash his
followers' feet. The text says he "took off his outer garments,"
and as I explained in chapter 3, some scholars think a relatively
poor man like Jesus may well not have had *inner* garments. So
when he took off his outer garments, that was a way of saying he
was naked, or nearly. Nudity is a sign of vulnerability, and this
is what the Gospel account conveys about the Son of God, who
"did not come to be served but to serve and to give his life as a
ransom for many" (Matthew 20:28). In complete vulnerability,
Jesus bends down and washes the dirty feet of his faithful yet
foolhardy disciples, including the one who would betray him
to his death. He gives his followers—including us—a graphic
glimpse at what living for others really means; in more ways
than one, it is dirty work.

Jesus' act of washing the disciples' feet, exceptional as it was, merely foreshadowed the ultimate self-sacrificial act that was to come the following day: the cross. His persecution and death show us where our eucharistic values will lead us, too, some day: to our own figurative and even sometimes literal crosses. Sr. Dorothy Stang, a Sister of Notre Dame de Namur and native of Dayton, Ohio, left her comfortable Midwestern home as a young sister to work alongside poor, marginalized farming families in the rainforests of Brazil. She served these farmers for almost forty years, teaching them sustainable practices and becoming one of them. Dorothy even became entangled in land disputes with powerful cattle ranchers, loggers, and others who had little regard for the land or the poor farmers' rights. Sr. Dorothy was the voice of these poor ones, speaking up for them, and she was their constant support when their crops were maliciously destroyed by their opponents.

For her insistence on telling the truth, supporting the poor, and preserving the land, Sr. Dorothy began to receive threats of death. She was getting older; she could have retired from this increasingly dangerous work and gone home to Ohio. But Sr. Dorothy stayed. On February 12, 2005, Sr. Dorothy and a farmer friend were walking along the road when hired gunmen stepped out of the forest and took aim. Sr. Dorothy reached in her bag and pulled out her Bible. She read from Jesus' Sermon on the Mount: blessed are those who hunger and thirst for justice....They shot Sr. Dorothy six times, killing her.

Unfortunately for those who hired these hit men, killing Sr. Dorothy did not make their troubles go away. Soon the United States government and many other powerful organizations became interested in a situation that led to the murder of an American nun, and other voices came to replace Sr. Dorothy's on behalf of the rainforest and the farmers. Eventually the Brazilian government would place 20,000 square miles of the rainforest—the heart of where Sr. Dorothy lived and worked—under federal protection.[124] Sr. Dorothy has become a beacon of inspiration for human rights and environmental workers around the globe. It seems in Sr. Dorothy's death, as in Christ's, there is resurrection.

Not all of us, thankfully, are called to literally give our lives for our faith in Christ. But every day, we who live the Eucharist feel both the joy and the pain, the dying and rising, of the life it calls us to lead: a life of love, of justice, of sacrifice. Sometimes this joy and pain are intermingled, inseparable, like a friendship with someone rejected by others, in whom one finds both treasure and burden. Or like speaking the truth when others will not, which can bring embarrassment and discomfort, but also assurance and peace after a friend privately expresses gratitude for your courage. One thing is for sure: Living a life steeped in the Eucharist is not comfortable and easy all the time. If it is, you're doing something wrong.

But living the liturgy has consequences that extend well beyond our personal, individual lives. Living a eucharistic life, a life formed and fed by the liturgy, takes us far, far beyond ourselves. Like Sr. Dorothy Stang, it may even lead us to serve our "neighbors" in other lands and cultures, for as Pope John Paul II put it, "the Eucharist is not merely an expression of communion in the Church's life; it is also a *project of solidarity* for all of humanity."[125] He goes on to say that every Mass has a universal character, which pulls us far beyond ourselves and calls us to be promoters of peace and dialogue among diverse peoples and cultures. If we are to alleviate the troubles, injustices, and deficiencies of our world, the Holy Father says we must "experience the Eucharist as a great school of peace, forming men and women who, at various levels of responsibility in social, cultural, and political life, can become promoters of dialogue and communion."[126] It is for this work, this fight for justice and peace, that we are sanctified in the liturgy.

An early twentieth-century American liturgical scholar and Benedictine monk named Virgil Michel, writing around the pinnacle of the liturgical movement, just before the reforms of Vatican II, made some bold claims about the liturgy. He thought the people of God, properly worshiping him through their full, conscious, and active participation in the liturgy, could transform our entire society. He saw Mass as the cooperative act *par excellence*, which could inspire a social culture built on loving cooperation and resulting in peace and justice for all. But he saw this wondrous result as dependent upon the full, conscious, and active participation of the faithful in liturgy. He called this spiritual communion of the faithful in worship by St. Paul's ancient term: the mystical body of Christ. He set out to achieve this world-transforming goal through his own scholarship and teaching on the liturgy, and the promotion of resources for educating Catholics about our worship, as a model for society. He was convinced that the liturgy was *the* model for social regeneration.

What if he was right?

Liturgist Karen Kane says, fifty years since the Second Vatican Council, one could argue we are finally "getting it" with regard to celebrating the liturgy.[127] In the decades that followed the council, we stabbed around in the dark with mixed results, looking for parameters within the new-found freedom it gave our celebrations. Here in North America there was bad music, even worse dancing, unfortunate banners, and even a couple of stray clowns in the sanctuary. Kane says we've come a long way from those days, and I agree. Don't get me wrong—I am not suggesting we have "arrived" when it comes to Mass. Liturgy today, like the humans who celebrate it, is certainly not perfect, but thanks to helpful directives by our bishops and a firm hand (even when we didn't want it) by the Vatican, we are hitting our stride when it comes to the Mass. Through strong, successful, and continuing efforts at educating priests, liturgists, musicians, ministers, and the faithful, Kane says we have begun to understand ourselves as God made us: his Church, joined by Christ to the Father in this sacrifice of praise and thanksgiving. Even you—yes, you with this book in your hands!—are contributing to the growing awareness, appreciation, and effectiveness of the Mass by learning more about it and your own important role therein.

And so I ask again, what if Dom Virgil Michel was right? What if a slow, graceful, lasting transformation of our world into one where peace and justice reign under the inspiration of the liturgy, fully lived, is happening right now?

Ite, missa est. Deo Gratias!

DISCUSSION QUESTIONS

1. *How does the Concluding Rite of Mass send worshipers forth into the world? What does it send them forth to do?*

2. *Is it significant to you that the name "Mass" is derived from the words of dismissal—from what Mass sends us forth to do in the world? Why or why not?*

3. *Are you surprised to learn that the concluding song has no official place in the Catholic Mass? Do you think it should? Why or why not?*

4. *What are the "values" of the Eucharist we celebrate? Besides the ways the author mentions, how can we live these values in the world? How can we live them, even when it is "dirty work?"*

5. *Do you think the liturgy could serve as a model for a just and peaceful society? Why or why not?*

Appendix:
The Third Edition of *The Roman Missal* and the New Translation of the Mass

On the weekend of November 26–27, 2011, many English-speaking Catholics, especially those in North America, began to use a new edition of The Roman Missal, which contains a new translation of the Mass. While no rituals or actions of the Mass changed, the words we use to pray the Mass were altered considerably in the new translation. Most notably, instead of responding, "And also with you" to the presider's liturgical greeting ("The Lord be with you"), many assemblies in the English-speaking world began to respond, "And with your spirit." There were many other minor and major adjustments to the prayers and dialogues of the Mass, and it took a while for the new words to sound and feel comfortable to the worshiping faithful. Many are still working through the changes. This appendix will seek to explain why Catholics received a new Missal, what was new about it, and the rationale behind the new translation, which brought the most significant changes to Catholic worship since the Second Vatican Council.

Before we go further, let's clarify what we mean when we say *"The Roman Missal."* The *Missale Romanum*, or in English, *The Roman Missal*, is a book containing the prayers and chants for Mass, and the instructions on how to perform the many rites that make up the Mass. (These instructions are called rubrics because they are printed in red type, and the Latin word for red is *rubeo*). The first officially mandated *Missal* was compiled around the Council of Trent in 1545 and also contained the readings for Mass. (To keep the physical size of the book manageable, the readings were eventually separated into their own volume: a book we call the *Lectionary.*) Although we can date the first official edition of *The Roman Missal* to the sixteenth century, many of the prayers the *Missal* contains are much older than that. In fact, the majority of the prayers contained in *The Roman Missal* are at least 1,000 years old, and many are much older.

Since the Second Vatican Council, the Church has promulgated three editions of *The Roman Missal.* The first was in 1970 and reflected the liturgical reforms of the council. The second was five years later and contained some rubrical changes to the 1970 edition. The Third Edition of *The Roman Missal* was released in the jubilee year of 2000 by Pope John Paul II. This newest edition of *The Roman Missal* is something like a content upgrade to the last edition; there are no very significant ritual changes. Prayers and texts were added for the celebration of Masses for newly canonized saints such as Padre Pio, and the Third Edition includes new texts for Vigil Masses on important feasts like the Assumption, Epiphany, and Pentecost. The new *Missal* itself was not the main cause for the changes to the words Catholics pray in the Mass. No, the reason for the changes had more to do with translation.

Each edition of *The Roman Missal* is first released in Latin, the ancient and venerable language of the Roman Catholic Church. Recall that until the 1970 edition of *The Roman Missal*, this book needed no translation. Until that time, the Church everywhere prayed the Mass in Latin, and the issue of translation did not come into play. However, Vatican II changed this reality, to the profound benefit of the worshiping faithful.

With this great gift of praying the Mass in our own languages came also a great challenge: the challenge of translation. If you've ever studied a foreign language, perhaps you understand something of this challenge. Sometimes translation is easy, and there exists in one language a one-to-one equivalent of what you are trying to say in another language. More often, however, this is not the case. Sometimes there is no equivalent word or phrase for the meaning you are trying to convey, so interpretation is needed. Sometimes a literal translation of words from one language becomes a popular phrase in another language and carries connotations you do not wish to suggest. Supreme facility with the languages involved is an absolute must for performing translations so that the very best choices are made and meaning is preserved.

And what are the very best choices in translating? Should a translator seek to capture the gist or overall meaning of a sentence or passage in translating it or aim for a translation that is more literal, paralleling words and phrases with all possible precision, even if the resultant language is less graceful? Regarding translation of the Mass, this has been the very question debated by Church scholars and officials in the generations following the Second Vatican Council. First we tried the first approach: a method of translation called "dynamic equivalence." This method, espoused in a 1969 instruction called *Comme le prevoit*, seeks to capture the overall meaning of the prayers and other texts for Mass, acknowledging that Latin has a different grammatical style and certain idiomatic phrases that are not easy to convey in English (and other languages). So, in accordance with the dynamic equivalence method of the 1969 instruction, the phrase, "*Et cum spiritu tuo*" was translated, "And also with you." To English ears, "And also with you" sounded more consistent with how we might typically respond to a greeting than the more literal translation, "And with your spirit." This overarching approach of dynamic equivalence resulted in very fluid, simple, and concise translations of the *Missal* for English-speaking Catholics. Various regions, like the United States and the United Kingdom, each had their own slightly different English translations, and these translations served English-speaking Catholics well for more than forty years.

However, there was a growing sentiment, especially at the Vatican, that English-speaking Catholics needed a new translation of the Mass, and the Church needed a new approach to translation in general. The clean, concise, dynamic equivalent translation we had been using for decades had never been intended for permanent use by the Church. The translations were completed quickly so that Vatican II's vision of the vernacular Mass could be realized in parish life. And while they served the Church well in their time, these early translations had the tendency to truncate the original Latin prayers, even "watering down" the Latin texts in some places, for the sake of fluidity in English. Other languages' translations, like Spanish and French, seemed much more faithful to the original Latin (although Spanish and French have the benefit of being Latin-derived languages, so translation is somewhat easier in their cases).

What's more, Catholics all over the world—from China to Ghana—often, if unofficially, use the English translation of *The Roman Missal* as a base text for translation into their languages, instead of the original Latin text. Why? Because many more scholars of English, capable of the tough work of translation, exist in the world (especially in the developing world) than do scholars of Latin. And if the English translation is a watered-down version of the Latin *Missale Romanum*, what will that mean for resultant translations based on the English? Church officials felt strongly that the Church cannot afford to play "telephone" with the liturgy, if we truly believe it is the source and summit of our lives as Christians.

All these realities convinced the Holy Father and other Vatican officials that the time was right for a new way of translating and a new translation of the Mass. In 2001, just a year after the announcement of a new *Missal*, the Holy See issued new guidelines for the translation of liturgical texts in a document called *Liturgiam Authenticam*. These guidelines departed from the dynamic equivalence method espoused by Church translators in the 1960s and insisted instead on a more literal, word-for-word approach to translation, with a strong emphasis on fidelity to the received texts. This method is known as "*formal* equivalence."

And so with a different approach to translation, scholars set out to translate the Third Edition of *The Roman Missal* into one English translation that all English-speaking Catholics would use. (You will note this is a change from the past practice of having multiple, slightly different translations of the Mass in English.) Their work and the process of approving it through official channels took more than ten years, but finally, on the First Sunday of Advent in 2011, English-speaking Catholics in several countries began to pray with a new translation of the Mass. Other English-speaking Catholics throughout the world have or will implement the new translation in the coming years.

There are many advantages to the new translation of the Mass. Because the translation method of formal equivalence used to produce it insists on a strong fidelity to the original text, in the new translation we actually enjoy more content from the Latin texts in the resultant prayers. Here is an example of what I mean, shown in a comparison between the Collect Prayer for the Feast of Epiphany from the Second and Third Editions of *The Roman Missal*.

Second Edition (1975):	**Third Edition (2011):**
Father,	O God, who on this day revealed your Only Begotten Son to the nations by the guidance of a star,
you revealed your Son to the nations by the guidance of a star.	
Lead us to your glory in heaven by the light of faith.	grant in your mercy that we, who know you already by faith, may be brought to behold the beauty of your sublime glory.
We ask this through our Lord…	Through our Lord…

Another example, this time from the twenty-seventh Sunday in ordinary time, also points up the increased content of the Third Edition's prayer texts:

Second Edition (1975):	Third Edition (2011):
Father,	Almighty ever-living God,
your love for us surpasses all our hopes and desires.	who in the abundance of your kindness surpass the merits and the desires of those who entreat you,
Forgive our failings, keep us in your peace, and lead us in the way of salvation.	pour out your mercy upon us to pardon what conscience dreads and to give what prayer does not dare to ask.
Grant this through our Lord...	Through our Lord...

Latin is a very compact language, full of nuances, and, in its more literal approach, the new translation captures more shades of meaning from the original text. What we gain in the new translation are richer theological and spiritual images, such as that from the second example Collect: God as boundlessly merciful, forgiving, and granting even that which we humans feel too low to admit or ask.

This brings up another difference between the old and new translations. At the time the former translation was conducted, in many circles of the Church there was a concern for bringing a somewhat personally disengaged faithful closer to God and perhaps for softening the image of God portrayed by the Church. This concern may have influenced the former translation of the Mass, for in it we find many references to "Father" (instead of "God," which is the literal translation of the more often used Latin word "*Deus*"). Also, the tone of supplication that runs through the original Latin texts was substantially softened in the former translation. Supplication means humbly asking for help, and having such a tone means *begging* for God's mercy and *pleading* for our human needs. It's a tone you adopt toward someone who is *obviously much greater* (in God's case, infinitely greater!) than you. This tone is restored in the new translation, and thus we find Collect prayers such as this one, from the ninth Sunday in ordinary time:

O God,
whose providence never fails in its design,
keep from us, we humbly beseech you,
all that might harm us
and grant all that works for our good.
Through our Lord Jesus Christ…

It is a source of debate among some Catholics whether this restored tone of supplication in the new translation of Mass is an advantage or a disadvantage. One's opinion on the matter may have to do with the culture surrounding the generation in which one was raised. Did your culture teach you that you are just a number, that you don't really matter much as an individual? Or did it teach you that one person can make all the difference in the world, that only the individual really matters? In our present culture, which tends to value the human individual, with its rights and privileges, even more than the common good (and doesn't even bring God up!), this supplicatory tone of the new *Missal* could be a strong advantage. The *Missal*'s tone helps to balance out the secular culture's overinflated sense of the individual's importance with proper reverence for God, on whom each individual, without distinction, is utterly dependent.

Besides its tone of supplication, the new translation of the Mass employs a more elevated style of language than the former translation. This is another feature of the new translation that was hotly debated in the months and years leading up to the new *Missal*'s implementation. Will the elevated language be a turn-off to the people in the pews? Will people without college educations (in my state, Ohio, that's three out of four) be able to understand words like "consubstantial," the word which, in the Nicene Creed, replaced "one in being" as a descriptor for the relationship between Father and Son? Proponents of this more elevated tone argue that in liturgy, we are doing something vastly different—and more elevated—than the rest of our weekly activities, and this elevated activity deserves elevated language to distinguish it as such. Yes, "consubstantial" is an unusual word, but the relationship between God the Father and God the Son that it describes is also quite unusual! Perhaps a word like "consubstantial" helps confront us on another level with the beautiful uniqueness of the truths of our faith.

Another advantage of the new translation is much less contentious: a stronger connection of the Mass to Scripture. With its more literal rendering of the Latin, the scriptural basis of our liturgical praying becomes much clearer in the new *Missal.* A classic example of this is the retranslation of the people's response to the presider's invitation to Communion: "Lord, I am not worthy that you should enter under my roof, but only say the word and my soul shall be healed." These words are taken from the Gospel of Luke, chapter 7, when Jesus is approached by a centurion whose beloved servant is near death. The centurion tells Jesus that he is not worthy to have Jesus come to his house, but being a man of power himself, he knows that if Jesus merely says the word, his servant will be healed. Of course Jesus does say the word, and the servant is healed. The story is less about unworthiness and more about the centurion's great faith: faith in the effective power of the Word-Made-Flesh. We are invited to show the same faith as we approach the eucharistic table. Such scriptural gems as this one are sprinkled throughout the new words we pray in the Third Edition of *The Roman Missal.* With this scriptural emphasis of the new translation, the Second Vatican Council's goal of opening the Scriptures more fully for the faithful is further realized with grace and in keeping with our ancient traditions of worship.

Even with its advantages, this new translation of the Mass presented challenges to English-speaking Catholics. Changes to Mass are always difficult and uncomfortable because our ways of worship are so ingrained in us. But so far, in most places, Catholics have survived and thrived with the new translation. The real spiritual impact of the Third Edition of *The Roman Missal* and the new English translation of the Mass remains to be seen. Time and the Holy Spirit will help us discern the real effectiveness of our words for worship. In most places, however, the implementation of the new *Missal* gave the faithful the opportunity to grow in understanding and appreciation for the Mass we celebrate as Catholics. Catechetical efforts in many places, conducted in preparation of the new *Missal*, were strenuous and well-received. Along with the new words for our celebration, these efforts toward greater understanding have been a great gift to the English-speaking Church.

For more information, listen to "Beyond the Words," a podcast series, co-hosted by the present author, all about the Third Edition of *The Roman Missal* and the new translation of the Mass. "Beyond the Words" is available for download through iTunes, or to stream online, visit beyondthewords.libsyn.com.

Endnotes

1 Vatican II, Constitution on the Sacred Liturgy (*Sacrosanctum Concilium*), ¶6.

2 Geoffrey Wainwright, *Doxology: The Praise and Worship of God in Worship, Doctrine, and Life* (New York: Oxford University Press, 1984), 224–225.

3 Mark S. Massa, *Catholics and American Culture: Fulton Sheen, Dorothy Day, and the Notre Dame Football Team* (New York: Crossroad, 1999), 156–157.

4 Emile Durkheim, *The Elementary Forms of the Religious Life*, 4th ed., trans. Joseph Ward Swain (London: George Allen & Unwin, 1957), 416. See also Mark S. Massa, *Catholics and American Culture: Fulton Sheen, Dorothy Day, and the Notre Dame Football Team*, 157.

5 Massa, *Catholics and American Culture*, 158.

6 Kathleen Harmon, *The Ministry of Music: Singing the Paschal Mystery* (Collegeville, MN: Liturgical Press, 2004), 8–9.

7 Vatican Council II, Constitution on the Sacred Liturgy (*Sacrosanctum Concilium*), ¶106.

8 Paul F. Bradshaw and Maxwell E. Johnson, *The Eucharistic Liturgies: Their Evolution and Interpretation* (Collegeville, MN: Liturgical Press, 2012), 26.

9 Adolf Adam, *The Liturgical Year: Its History and Its Meaning After the Reform of the Liturgy* (Collegeville, MN: Liturgical Press, 1990), 37.

10 Dom Gregory Dix, *The Shape of the Liturgy* (London: Dacre Press, Adam and Charles Black, 1945), 148.

11 Bradshaw and Johnson, *The Eucharistic Liturgies*, 24.

12 Robert F. Taft, "Mass Without the Consecration?" *America* (May 12, 2003), online version found at americamagazine. org, accessed May 7, 2012.

13 Theodor Klauser, *A Short History of the Western Liturgy*, trans. John Halliburton (London: Oxford University Press, 1969), 5.

14 Kenneth W. Stevenson, *The First Rites: Worship in the Early Church* (Collegeville, MN: Liturgical Press, 1990), 25.

15 Dix, *The Shape of the Liturgy*, 141.

16 *Ibid.*, 143.

17 Edward Foley, *Foundations of Christian Music: the Music of Pre-Constantinian Christianity* (Collegeville, MN: Liturgical Press, 1996), 6.

18 Edward Foley, *From Age to Age: How Christians Have Celebrated the Eucharist* (Chicago: Liturgy Training Publications, 1991), 32.

19 Joseph Gelineau, "Music and Singing in the Liturgy," in *The Study of Liturgy*, ed. Cheslyn Jones *et al.* (New York: Oxford University Press, 1978), 440.

20 Dix, *The Shape of the Liturgy*, 142.

21 Foley, *From Age to Age*, 26.

22 Klauser, *A Short History of the Western Liturgy*, 33.

23 *Ibid.*, 35.

24 Peter Brown, *The World of Late Antiquity: AD 150-750* (New York: W.W. Norton & Co., 1989), 82.

25 Foley, *From Age to Age*, 68.

26 Klauser, *A Short History of the Western Liturgy*, 9.

27 Foley, *From Age to Age*, 79.

28 Eamon Duffy, *The Stripping of the Altars: Traditional Religion in England, 1400–1580* (New Haven, CT: Yale University Press, 1992), 52.

29 John Bossy, *Christianity in the West: 1400–1700* (Oxford, UK: Oxford University Press, 1985), 14–21, 49.

30 Foley, *From Age to Age*, 116.

31 Steven Ozment, *The Age of Reform 1250–1550: An Intellectual and Religious History of Late Medieval and Reformation Europe* (New Haven, CT: Yale University Press, 1981), 436.

32 Klauser, *A Short History of the Western Liturgy*, 119.

33 *Ibid.*, 121.

34 J.D. Crichton, *Lights in the Darkness: Forerunners of the Liturgical Movement* (Collegeville, MN: The Liturgical Press, 1996), 152.

35 Kathleen Hughes, RSCJ, ed. *How Firm a Foundation: Voices of the Early Liturgical Movement* (Chicago: Liturgy Training Publications, 1990), 25.

36 Joseph Ratzinger, "The First Session," *Worship* 37 (August–September 1963), 530–535.

37 Frederick R. McManus, "Liturgical Reform of Vatican II," in *The New Dictionary of Sacramental Worship*, ed. Peter E. Fink, SJ (Collegeville, MN: Liturgical Press, 1990), 1084.

38 Vatican II, Constitution on the Sacred Liturgy (*Sacrosanctum Concilium*), ¶10.

39 *Ibid.*, ¶11.

40 *Ibid.*, ¶14.

41 *Ibid.*, ¶37.

42 *Ibid.*, ¶14.

43 *Ibid.*, ¶11. Emphasis added.

44 Some of these fine answers, indeed much of my own overarching articulation of the phrase "paschal mystery," come from James L. Empereur, SJ's short but wonderful article "Paschal Mystery" from *The New Dictionary of Theology*, ed. Joseph A. Komonchak *et al.* (Collegeville, MN: Liturgical Press, 1987), 744–747. I owe much to this article for both the structure and content of the rest of chapter 3.

45 Pope Benedict XVI, *Sacramentum Caritatis*, ¶10. Emphasis added.

46 *Ibid.*, ¶9.

47 Vatican II, Constitution on the Sacred Liturgy (*Sacrosanctum Concilium*), ¶47.

48 *Ibid.*, ¶48

49 *The General Instruction of the Roman Missal*, 2011, ¶93.

50 *Ibid.*, ¶95.

51 U.S. Conference of Catholic of Bishops, *Built of Living Stones: Art, Architecture, and Worship* (Washington: USCCB, 2001), ¶97.

52 *The General Instruction of The Roman Missal*, 2011, ¶46.

53 *Ibid.*

54 *Ibid.*, ¶47.

55 Lawrence J. Johnson, *The Mystery of Faith: A Study of the Structural Elements of the Order of the Mass* (FDLC: Washington, D.C., 2003), 3.

56 Vatican Council II, The Dogmatic Constitution on the Church (*Lumen Gentium*), 1964, ¶8.

57 *The General Instruction of The Roman Missal*, 2011, ¶50.

58 Johnson, *The Mystery of Faith*, 11.

59 *The General Instruction of The Roman Missal*, 2011, ¶51.

60 Johnson, *The Mystery of Faith*, 13.

61 *The General Instruction of The Roman Missal*, 2011, ¶51.

62 *The General Instruction of The Roman Missal*, 2011, ¶54.

63 *Ibid.*

64 *The General Instruction of The Roman Missal*, 2011, ¶55.

65 R. Kevin Seasoltz, OSB, "Liturgy and Social Consciousness," in *To Do Justice And Right Upon The Earth: Papers From The Virgil Michel Symposium On Liturgy And Social Justice*, ed. Mary E. Stamps (Collegeville, MN: Liturgical Press, 1993), 43.

66 USCCB, *Lectionary for Mass: Introduction*, 1981, ¶10.

67 *The General Instruction of The Roman Missal*, 2011, ¶57.

68 St. Augustine, Sermon 272.

69 USCCB, *Lectionary for Mass: Introduction*, 1981, ¶3.

70 *The General Instruction of The Roman Missal*, 2011, ¶56.

71 *Ibid.*

72 Gabe Huck and Gerald T. Chinchar, *Liturgy With Style and Grace* (Chicago: Liturgy Training Publications, 1998), 74.

73 *The General Instruction of The Roman Missal*, 2011, ¶59.

74 *Ibid.*, ¶61.

75 *Lectionary for Mass: Introduction*, 1981, ¶23.

76 *Ibid.*, ¶24.

77 *Ibid.*

78 *Ibid.*, ¶28.

79 *The General Instruction of The Roman Missal*, 2011, ¶68.

80 Nicholas Lash, *Believing Three Ways in One God: A Reading of the Apostles' Creed* (Notre Dame, IN: University of Notre Dame Press, 1993), 9, etc.

81 *The General Instruction of The Roman Missal*, 2011, ¶69.

82 *Ibid.*, ¶70.

83 Johnson, *The Mystery of Faith*, 51.

84 *Lectionary for Mass: Introduction*, 1981, ¶6.

85 *The General Instruction of The Roman Missal*, 2011, ¶72.

86 Frank Senn, "Anamnesis" from *The New Dictionary of Sacramental Worship*, ed. Peter E. Fink, SJ (Collegeville, MN: Liturgical Press, 1990), 45.

87 Johnson, *The Mystery of Faith*, 58.

88 USCCB, *Built of Living Stones*, 2000, ¶56.

89 *The General Instruction of The Roman Missal*, 2011, ¶73.

90 *Ibid.*

91 *The Roman Missal*, Third Edition, ¶23–24.

92 Johnson, *The Mystery of Faith*, 68.

93 *The General Instruction of The Roman Missal*, 2011, ¶75.

94 USCCB, *Sing to the Lord: Music in Divine Worship*, 2007, ¶142, 173.

95 Johnson, *The Mystery of Faith*, 73.

96 John Barry Ryan, "Eucharistic Prayers," from *The New Dictionary of Sacramental Worship*, ed. Peter E. Fink, SJ (Collegeville, MN: The Liturgical Press, 1990), 452. I am very grateful to this article as a whole for helping to organize my discussion of the Eucharistic Prayer.

97 Archdiocese of Cincinnati, *Beyond the Words* podcast, Episode 13, "The People's New Words Part III," interview with Fr. Tim Kallaher, released February 8, 2012.

98 Johnson, *The Mystery of Faith*, 80.

99 *The General Instruction of The Roman Missal*, 2011, ¶79.b.

100 *Ibid.*, ¶79.d.

101 *Ibid.*, ¶79.e.

102 *Ibid.*, ¶79.f.

103 *Ibid.*, ¶79.g.

104 *Ibid.*, ¶43.

105 *Ibid.*, ¶82.

106 *The Roman Missal*, Third Edition.

107 *Ibid.*

108 USCCB, *Sing to the Lord*, 2007, ¶191.

109 *The General Instruction of The Roman Missal*, 2011, ¶86.

110 USCCB, *Sing to the Lord*, 2007, ¶189.

111 Boniface Ramsey, ed., *The Works of St. Augustine*, Part III, *Essential Sermons*, trans. Edmund Hill, O.P. (Hyde Park, NY: New City Press, 2007), 317-318.

112 *The General Instruction of The Roman Missal*, 2011, ¶89.

113 *The Roman Missal*, Third Edition, ¶141.

114 Gerald T. Chinchar, SM, "Liturgy Notes: The Missiology of the Concluding Rite of the Mass of the Roman Rite," in *Liturgical Ministry* (Winter 2002), 45.

115 R. Kevin Seasoltz, OSB, "Liturgy and Social Consciousness," in *To Do Justice and Right Upon the Earth: Papers From the Virgil Michel Symposium on Liturgy and Social Justice*, ed. Mary E. Stamps (Collegeville, MN: Liturgical Press, 1993), 42.

116 Chinchar, "Liturgy Notes: The Missiology of the Concluding Rite," 46.

117 *The Roman Missal*, Third Edition, Solemn Blessings, ¶12.

118 *Ibid.*, ¶4.

119 Dennis Sadowski, "New dismissal options at Mass meant to help people live the Gospel," Catholic News Service, October 24, 2008, accessed January 4, 2013, catholicnews.com/data/stories/cns/0805441.htm.

120 USCCB, *Sing to the Lord*, 2007, ¶199.

121 Chinchar, "Liturgy Notes: The Missiology of the Concluding Rite," 46.

122 John Paul II, *Mane nobiscum Domine*, 2004, ¶24. Emphasis original to text.

123 *Ibid.*, ¶25.

124 Website of the Sisters of Notre Dame de Namur, Ohio, sndohio.org/sister-dorothy/Expanded-Story.cfm, accessed November 20, 2012.

125 John Paul II, *Mane nobiscum Domine*, 2004, ¶27. Emphasis original to text.

126 *Ibid.*

127 Karen Kane, "Liturgy Paves the Road to Gospel Living," in *Pastoral Music* (December–January 2008), 18.

CPSIA information can be obtained at www.ICGtesting.com
Printed in the USA
LVOW10s0107300716

498134LV00012B/108/P

9 780764 822254